Matters of the Heart and Soul

The Refinement of Character

(Book 1 of 4)

Ibn Qudamah
Ibn Al-Jawzi
Ibn Kathir

Matters of the Heart and Soul

This work has taken Important Points and Objectives from The Minhaj Al-Qasidin of Ibn Al-Jawzi which in turn is a Summary of that Magnum Opus of Imam al-Ghazali. The 'Ihya Ulum Ad-Din'. However, Ibn Al-Jawzi Compiled the book free from weak or fabricated Hadith, Ibn QudamaH summarized it further, and Ibn Kathir added his invaluable comments. The Arabic is in one volume, however the English version comprises of 4 separate books

The First Book

Covers the ethics of eating, marriage, and companionship, earning a living, traveling, enjoying the good, and staying away from sin and evil deeds, as well the rulings on music and singing. It ends with heartfelt advice from our righteous predecessors and illustrates the beautiful character of our beloved Prophet Muhammad (peace and blessings be upon him).

Anyone who adorns themself with this Islamic Character will indeed achieve nobility of the elite of Allah's creation, which is beloved to our Creator, Allah, the Most High.

"O Muslim, adorn and beautify yourself with great morals and manners."

The Second book

Ibn Qudamah (may Allah have mercy on him) discusses the marvels of the heart and curing the sickness therein, disciplining the self, and breaking the desire of the stomach and the private parts. It also covers how to deal with pride, malice, envy, and the defects of the tongue. It concludes with the harms of greed, the praise of wealth, showing off, self-delusion, and how to overcome all these diseases that harm the spirituality of any person that is seeking the Hereafter.

Ibn Qudamah (may Allah have mercy on him) discusses the marvels of the heart and curing the sickness therein, disciplining the self, and breaking the desire of the stomach and the private parts. It also covers how to deal with pride, malice, envy, and the defects of the tongue. It concludes with the harms of greed, the praise of wealth, showing off, self-delusion, and how to overcome all these diseases that harm the spirituality of any person that is seeking the Hereafter.

The Third book

Imam Ibn Qudamah sets out the importance of worship and how worship has to be done with the knowledge of the Quran and Sunnah, as well as giving examples of our pious predecessors. It covers many aspects of worship, such as Knowledge, Purification, Prayer, Zakat, Fasting, Hajj, Reciting the Quran, supplications, and the excellence of the Night Prayer.

The Fourth book

The author Imam Ibn Qudamah al-Maqdisi - may Allah have mercy on him - discusses how to purify the soul and remove the rust of desire and heedlessness which encapsulates the heart. He quotes from the Qur'an, Sunnah, the Companions of the Prophet (peace and blessings be upon him) and stories from the salaf.

This set is one of the best companions for a Muslims Journey through the World

Book 1: Matters of the Heart and Soul: The Refinement of Character
Book 2: Matters of the Heart and Soul: The Path to Spiritual Growth
Book 3: Matters of the Heart and Soul: The Inner Secrets of Worship
Book 4: Matters of the Heart and Soul: Purification of the Soul

And indeed, you are of a great moral character.
(68:4)

وَإِنَّكَ لَعَلَىٰ خُلُقٍ عَظِيمٍ ٤

Content

AUTHOR'S INTRODUCTION.......11

CHAPTER ONE
On the Ethics of Eating
(*kitāb ādāb al-akl*).......13

The first category: This pertains to the etiquette before eating.......13

The second category: This pertains to the etiquette during eating.......14

The third category: This pertains to the recommended etiquette after eating.......16

1.1. The Manners of Eating When in Company with Others.......16

1.2. Manners to be adopted when Presenting Food to One's Brothers.......17

1.3. Not entering upon people who are Eating.......18

1.4. The Manners of Hospitality.......18

1.5. The Etiquette of Presenting the Food and Eating.......20

CHAPTER TWO
On the Ethics of Marriage
(*kitāb ādāb al-nikāḥ*)..22
2.1. The disadvantages of Marriage..24
2.2. Gracious Companionship..25
2.3. The Etiquette of Graceful Companionship and the Duties of Both Spouses..27

CHAPTER THREE
On the Ethics in Earning a Livelihood
(*Kitāb ādāb al-Kasb wa'l-Ma'āsh*)..34
3.1. On the Virtues of Work and Exhortation Towards It...34
First: On the Science of Valid Selling, Buying and Transactions...37
Second: On the Exposition of Justice (*al-'adl*) in Transactions, Avoiding Oppression and the Prohibition of Hoarding..39
Third: On the Exposition of benevolence (*al-iḥsān*) in Transactions...40
The fourth: On the Merchant's Concern for His Religion......41

CHAPTER FOUR
On the Ethics in the Lawful and the Unlawful
(*Kitāb al-ḥalāl wa'l-ḥarām*)..43
4.1. Exposition on the degrees of the Lawful and the Unlawful...45
4.2. Exposition on the degrees of Prudence..........................46
4.3. Exposition on the State of those who Socialise with Tyrannical Rulers 56
4.2. Going to tyrannical rulers Due to an Excuse..................58

CHAPTER FIVE
On the Ethics in Companionship and Brotherhood
(*Kitāb ādāb al-subba wa'l-akwa wa mu'asharat al-khalq*)............61
5.1. Exposition on What Must Be Considered When Choosing Companionship............65
5.2. Exposition on the Rights of Brotherhood and Companionship characteristics............68
5.3. Exposition on the Etiquettes of Interaction with People............75
5.4. The rights of Muslims, kinship, neighbours, kings.........77
5.5. The rights of the relatives and kinsmen............84

CHAPTER SIX
On the Ethics of Solitude
(*Kitāb ādāb al-'uzla*)............86
6.1. On the Benefits of Solitude, and its Pitfalls, and showing the truth about the superiority of solitude...89
6.2. On the Pitfalls of Solitude............95
6.2. Etiquettes of Solitude............101

CHAPTER SEVEN
On the Ethics in Travelling
(*Kitāb ādāb al-safr*)............103
7.1. On Permissible Travelling............106
7.2. On what the Traveller must do............108

CHAPTER EIGHT
On the Ethics of Enjoining Good and Forbidding Evil
(*Kitāb al-amr bi'l-ma'rūf wa'l-nahyī 'an'l-munkar*)............110
8.1. On the Stages of Enjoining Good and Forbidding Evil............112
8.2. On the Pillars, Conditions, Levels and Etiquettes on Enjoining Good and Forbidding Evil............113
8.3. The Stages of Guarding against infringements............115

8.4. On the Qualities of the person engaged in preventing Infringements......124

CHAPTER NINE
On the Reprehensible Actions which people are accustomed to, and enjoining rulers to do good and forbidding them from doing evil......127
9.1. Reprehensible Actions......127
[i] The reprehensible actions of the masajids......127
[ii] Reprehensible actions in the markets......128
[iii] Reprehensible acts in the streets......129
[iv] Reprehensible actions in bathhouses......130
[v] Reprehensible actions in hosting people......130
[iv] General reprehensible actions......131
9.2. Enjoining Rulers and Sultans to do good and prohibiting them from doing evil......132

CHAPTER TEN
On the Ruling of Listening to (Music and) Singing (*Fasl fi hukm al-samā' wa'l-ghinā'*)......149

CHAPTER ELEVEN
The Conduct of Life as Exemplified by the Prophetic Character (*Kitāb ādāb ma'isha wa akhlāq al-Nubuwwa*)......153
11.1. A Summary Account of His (ﷺ) Manner and Character......155
11.2. A Summary Account of His (ﷺ) Miracles......158

Introduction

In the Name of Allah, the Most Beneficent, Most Merciful

Shaykh *al-Imām, al-Zāhid, al-'Ābid, al-Awhad al-'Allāmah* Najmuddīn Abu'l-'Abbās Aḥmad ibn Shaykh *al-Imām al-'Ālim al-'Āmil al-Zāhid al-'Ābid al-'Allāmah* 'Izzuddīn Abū 'Abdullāh Muḥammad Ibn Shaykh *al-Imām al- 'Ālim al-'Āmil al-Zāhid al-'Ābid al-' Allāmah Shaykh ul-Islām Mufti ul-Anām, Sayyid ul-'Ulama wa'l-Hukkām*, Shamsuddīn Abū Muḥammad 'Abdu'l-Raḥmān ibn *Shaykh al-Imām al-'Ālim al-'Āmil al-'Ārif al-Zāhid al-Wari' Shaykh ul-Islām* Abū 'Umar Muḥammad Ibn Aḥmad Ibn Muḥammad Ibn Qudāmah al-Maqdisī al-Ḥanbalī said:

All praise is due to Allāh Whose Mercy covers all of his servants and has specified those who have obedience with guidance to the path of guidance and has granted them, by His *Lutf* (Subtlety and Gentleness), to righteous actions and they have gained success by reaching the intent.

I praise Him, affirming the abundant aid which He imparts, and I seek refuge in Him from expulsion and distance [from Him]. I testify that there is no god worthy of worship except Allāh alone with no partner, a testimony which is stored for the Abode of Resurrection. I testify that Muḥammad is His servant and messenger who clarified the path of guidance and accuracy, suppressed the rejectors and deniers from the people of deviation and stubbornness. May Allāh's peace and blessings be upon him, to proceed:

One time I came across the book *Minhāj al-Qāṣidīn* by *Shaykh al-Imām al-ʿĀlim al-Awḥad*, Jamāl al-Dīn ibn al-Jawzī (*raḥimahullāh*) and I saw that it was of the most magnificent and beneficial of books containing many benefits. I came across at a certain location and I desired to obtain it and read through it. When I contemplated on it for a second time I found more than what I had thought was in it. However, I found that the book was simple and thus I wanted to comment on it in this *Mukhtaṣar* which will contain most of its intents and important aspects and benefits whether it be the clear issues mentioned in the beginning of it related to the *furūʿ*, as these are famous matters in the books of *fiqh* and known among the people, as the intent of the book is not to deal with those matters.[1]

I did not adhere to preserving the arrangement of the book and its specific terminologies, rather I mentioned some of them in a way and meaning so as to be brief. I may have mentioned a ḥadīth or something else which was relevant to it and Allāh knows best. I ask Allāh the Most Kind to bring benefit with it and from reading, listening or looking at it, and to make it sincerely for Allāh's Face, and to seal it with good for us; and to grant us success to whatever statements and actions please Him. And may Allāh overlook our shortcomings and our negligence, He is Sufficient for us and the Best Trustee of affairs.

[1] The intent of the book is as an admonishment, it is a work of heart softening (*raqāʾiq*), *sulūk* and actions of the heart (*aʿmal al-qulūb*).

Chapter One

On the Ethics of Eating

The etiquettes (*ādāb*) to be observed before eating, when eating and what is recommended after eating.

The first category: this pertains to the etiquette before eating

This includes washing the hands before eating as occurs in the ḥadīth,[1] for there is always some dirt on them.

The food should be placed on a *sufra* (ground cover) on the ground, for this is closer to the way of Allāh's Messenger (ﷺ) than raising it on a table (*mā'idah*)[2]. It is also more indicative of humbleness (*tawāda'*).

He should sit at the *sufra* (as it is spread on the ground), raising his right leg and sitting on his left. He should intend to eat in order

---

[1] Everything that has been narrated about this is weak as stated by al-Ḥāfiẓ al-'Irāqī in *Takhrīj al-Iḥyā'*, vol.2, p.3.

[2] Refer to *Mukhtaṣar al-Shamā'il al-Muḥammadiyya li'l-Tirmidhī* by our Shaykh, the erudite scholar al-Albānī, p. 88.

of strengthening oneself in obedience (*ṭā'at*) to Allāh, so as to be obedient through food and not to seek luxurious living only. A sign that this indeed is one's intention is when one only eats what suffices without filling his stomach. The Prophet (ﷺ) said: "No human being has ever filled a container worse than his own stomach. The son of Adam needs no more than some morsels of food to keep up his strength; doing so, he should consider that a third of [his stomach] is for food, one third for drink, and one third for breathing."[3]

A necessary requisite of this intention (*niyya*) is that one does not reach his hand towards the food if he is not hungry and lifts his hand before his is full. Doing so, he dispenses with doctors.

This etiquette also includes being content with any sustenance that is available, one he should not belittle it no matter how little the foods is and he should do his best to have many hands partake in the meal, even if it be just the hands of his spouse and children.

The second category: This pertains to the etiquette during eating

He should begin the meal with the words '*In the name of Allāh*' and end it with praising Allāh. He should eat with the right hand, take small morsels, and chew his food well. He should not stretch his hand to take another mouthful before swallowing the first and not criticize the food.

He should eat of that which is the closest to him, unless the food is of different types like fruits. He should eat with three fingers, and if food falls on the ground he should pick it up.

[3] Tirmidhī #2381; Aḥmad, vol.3, p.132; Ibn Mājah #3349; al-Baghawī #4048; Ibn Hibbān #1349 (*Mawarid*); Ibn al-Mubārak in *al-Zuhd* #603; Ṭabarānī in *al-Kabir*, vol.20, p.272-273; and Ḥākim, vol.4, p.121 with a ṣaḥīḥ isnād.

He should not blow on hot food [rather wait patiently until it is easy to eat].

He must not place dates and their stones together in one dish or bring them together in the palm of the hand, but should place stones from his mouth into his palm of the hand and then discard them. This applies to everything with stones or seeds similarly.

A person should not drink [much] while eating as this is medical desired.

As for the manners of drinking, he should take the vessel with the right hand; and he should look into the vessel before drinking. He should drink it in sips rather than in gulps, for it has been narrated that 'Alī (*raḍiy-Allāh 'anhu*) said: 'Drink water in sips, do not gulp it down, for liver ailments are brought about by gulping.'

One should not drink while standing up and should take three breaths when drinking.

It occurs in the Two Ṣaḥīḥs that the Prophet (ﷺ) used to breathe three times in a vessel.[4]

This ḥadīth means that he used to breathe while drinking from a vessel after taking it away from his mouth first, not that he breathed inside the vessel.

[4] Bukhārī, vol.10, p.81; Muslim #2028; Tirmidhī #1885; Abū Dāwūd #3727 on the authority of Anas (*raḍiy-Allāh 'anhu*).

The third category: This pertains to the recommended etiquette after eating

He should stop eating before becoming full and then lick his fingers. He then wipes the vessel[5] clean and praises Allāh. It is narrated that the Prophet (ﷺ) said: "Allāh is pleased that a servant eats something and then praises Him for it. Drinks something and then praises Him for it."[6] Then he should wash the smell of the meat and its grease from his hands.

Section One:

The Manners of Eating when in Company of Others

The first [rule of conduct] is one should not begin eating if he is with someone who deserves to commence because of his age or virtue. If, however, he himself is the role-model, he should be the one who begins.

The second [rule of conduct] is that they should not eat in silence but should instead converse about good things. For example, they can relate the stories of the pious regarding food.[7]

The third [rule of conduct] is each person should prefer the other over himself and should not let his companion feel the need to say: "Eat!" One should eat cheerfully and not act pretentiously by holding back.

[5] The Arabic word for vessel here is *"qaṣ'a"* It says in the Shāmiyyah edition: *"qaṣṣa"* which is an error.

[6] Muslim #2734; Tirmidhī #1817 on the authority of Anas (*raḍiy-Allāh 'anhu*).

[7] What is correct regarding this and other matters are the words of Allāh's Messenger (ﷺ): "Whoever believes in Allāh and the last day, let him speak good or remain silent." Narrated by Muslim #48 on the authority of Abū Shurayḥ (*raḍiy-Allāh 'anhu*).

The fourth [rule of conduct] is that one should not look directly at his companions as they eat so that they do not become embarrassed.

The fifth [rule of conduct] is that he should refrain from anything he himself would find repulsive, such as shaking what is on his hand into the vessel and putting his head above it when putting a morsel in his mouth. If he needs to take something from his mouth and throw it away, he should turn his face elsewhere and take it with his left hand. He does not dip a greasy morsel into the vinegar nor pour vinegar on something greasy as others may not like that. He must not dip a morsel he has already eaten from into the broth.

Section Two:

Manners to be adopted when Presenting Food to One's Brothers

It is recommended to offer food to one's brothers. It has been narrated that 'Alī (*raḍiyAllāh 'anhu*) said: "Gathering my brothers to eat a *ṣā*[8] of food is more beloved to me than freeing a slave."

Khaythama would prepare *Khabiṣ*[9] and fine food and then invite Ibrāhīm and al-A'mash and say: "Eat, for I have only prepared it for you."

Regarding the manners of presenting food, he should present the food that is available without going overboard and should not ask for their permission to do so. One way of going overboard is to offer everything that one has.

The good conduct of a visitor includes that he should neither sug-

[8] A unit of measurement which can vary.

[9] Sweets made of dates and butter.

gest nor demand any specific food. If, however, he is given a choice of two dishes, let him choose the easiest of the two (to prepare) unless he knows that his host is pleased with his suggestion and will gladly prepare it. Indeed, al-Shāfi'ī once went to al- Za'farānī who used to write a list every day of the different varieties to be cooked that day and then give it to the servant-girl. Al-Shāfi'ī took the list and added a new variety to it, and when al-Za'farānī found out about this, he rejoiced greatly.

Section Three:
Not entering upon people who are Eating

Nobody should go to a people if he knows that they are currently eating. If he does not know this and then finds them eating, he should look at the situation if they tell him to join them: if he knows that they only asked him out of shyness, he should not eat, but if he knows that they really want to eat with him, he is permitted to eat.

If a person enters his friend's house and knows for sure that him eating his food would only make him happy, he is permitted to eat.

Section Four:
The Manners of Hospitality

The etiquette of hosting includes that one invites the pious (*atqiyā'*), not the shameless sinners (*fisāq*). One of the pious predecessors has said: "Only eat the food of a god-fearing person (*taqī*), and let only a god-fearing person (*taqī*) eat your food."[10]

He should also direct his invitation to the poor (*fuqarā'*) rather

[10] This has been narrated with a isnād going back to the Prophet (ﷺ) himself on the authority of Abū Sa'īd al-Khudrī (*raḍiy-Allāh 'anhu*). It was related by Abū Dāwūd #4832; Tirmidhī #2397; and Ibn Ḥibbān #2049 (*Mawārid*) with a ḥasan isnād.

than the rich.

He must not neglect his relatives when it comes to hosting as neglecting them leads to unfamiliarity and leads to the breaking of the ties of kinship.

He should observe an order (*tartīb*) in inviting his friends and acquaintances and must not invite people in order to brag (*mubāhāh*) and boast (*tafākhur*). His intention should be to implement the Sunnah of feeding others, uniting the hearts of his brothers, and bringing joy (*surūr*) into the hearts of the believers.

He should not invite people whom he knows have a hard time coming, or who might be harmed by others who attend for one reason or another.

With respect to the etiquette of accepting invitations, one is obliged to go when a Muslim invites him to a wedding on the first day, while accepting other invitations is permissible. One must not only accept the invitation of the rich and not go to the poor, and should not stay home if he is fasting; he should still go. Iif his fasting is voluntary and he knows that breaking it would make his Muslim brother happy, he should break it.

If the food is unlawful (*ḥarām*), he must not accept the invitation. The same applies if there is unlawful furniture or vessels, or flutes or unlawful images. Similarly, if the inviter is an oppressor (*ẓālim*), shameless sinner (*fāsiq*), innovator (*mubtadiʿ*), or someone who boasts (*mufākir*) with his invitations, one should not attend.

One should not answer an invitation just because of the food; rather, he should make the intention of following the Sunnah and honoring (*iqrām*) his Muslim brother. He should also intend to protect himself from the evil opinion (*ẓann*) of others as some might say he is arrogant (*mutakabir*) if he does not attend!

In the gathering, he should be humble and not seek a notable position. If the owner of the house appoints a specific place for him, he must not sit elsewhere. He must not gaze frequently at the place where the food is brought from as that is a sign of greed.

Section Five:
The Etiquette of Presenting the Food and Eating

As regarding the presentation of food, there are five rules of good conduct:

The first is that the food should be served quickly (*ta'jīl*), as that is a form of honoring the guest (*iqrām al-ḍaif*).

The second [rule of good conduct] is that, fruits should be presented first as that is better from the medical perspective. Allāh says:

وَفَٰكِهَةٍ مِّمَّا يَتَخَيَّرُونَ ﴿٢٠﴾ وَلَحْمِ طَيْرٍ مِّمَّا يَشْتَهُونَ ﴿٢١﴾

> "And fruit of what they select. And the meat of fowl, from whatever they desire."
>
> [*al-Wāqi'ah* (56):20-21]

After fruits, the best thing to present is meat, especially fried one. The best food after meat is *tharīd* (bread layered with lamb stew) then sweetmeat. These good provisions are completed with drinking cool water and the matter is sealed by washing the hands with lukewarm water.

The third [rule of good conduct] is that, all available varieties should be presented.

The fourth [rule of good conduct] is that a person should not hurry to remove the dishes before [the guests] have ceased to eat and have raised their hands.

The fifth [rule of good conduct] is that sufficient amount of food should be served, for serving too little indicates that one lacks good manners.

The host should put aside his family's share of the food before offering it.

When the guest wants to leave, the host should accompany him to the door as this is a Sunnah and a way of honoring the guest. A full show of respect (*tamām al-iqrām*) is completed by smiling and pleasant conversation when entering or leaving, and also at the table.

As for the guest, he should leave with a content heart even if he did not get his rights in full. This is a part of good character (*ḥusn al-khuluq*) and humility (*tawāḍi'*). He must only leave after the acceptance and permission of the permission of the owner of the house [the host] and he should examine his heart for the amount of time he may stay.

Chapter Two

On the Ethics of Marriage

The scholars do not differ about the fact that marriage is recommended (*mustaḥabb*) and entails many virtues. There are many benefits in it, including the following:

Children: marriage aims to preserve one's lineage. Making children also earns the love of Allāh as one helps the survival of mankind.

It is also a way of seeking the love of Allāh's Messenger (ﷺ) as one increases what is a source of glory for him.

It also entails seeking the blessings of the supplications of pious children and earning the intercession (*shafā'ah*) if a small child passes away.

It is also a way of protecting oneself from the Satan by repelling the perils of lust (*ghawā'il al-shahwa*).

It is also a way of relaxing the soul and keeping it company by interacting with one's wife.

It is also a way of empting the heart (*tafrigh al-qalb*) of the trouble of running the household, (and all the chores of) cooking and cleaning, furnishing, washing dishes, and preparing decent means of living. Constantly preoccupied with domestic chores alone is very difficult; it takes most of one's time and hinders him from studying and doing good deeds. A virtuous wife and good housekeeper is therefore an aid to helps one in practicing his religion in this way, for deficiency in carrying out these chores distract the heart.

It is also a way of striving against the soul (*mujāhadat al-nafs*) and training (*riyāḍah*) it through custodianship (*ri'āya*), guardianship (*wilāya*) and fulfilling the family's rights. One benefits from having patience (*ṣabr*) with his wife's manners and bearing her harm as he rectifies them and directs them to the religion's path. One also benefits from working and making a lawful living for her sake and raising the children. All of these are tremendously meritorious acts, for they constitute custodianship and guardianship.

One should only refrain from marriage if he fears that he might not be able to fulfill her rights. Bearing the burden of wife and children is like *jihād* in Allāh's path.

It occurs in the collection of Muslim that the Prophet (ﷺ) said: "A *dinār* you spent in Allāh's path, a *dinār* you spent to free a slave, a *dinar* you gave as charity to a poor person, and a *dinar* you spent on your family-the best of them is the one you spent on your family."[1]

[1] Muslim #995 on the authority of Abū Hurayrah (*raḍiy-Allah 'anhu*)

Section one:
The Disadvantages of Marriage

There are a number of drawbacks in marriage:

The first and the most serious drawback lies in the difficulty of lawful livelihood (*ḥalāl*)—it may be that the married person reaches his hand towards something that is not rightfully his [whereas the bachelor is safe from this].

The second drawback lies in the difficulty of giving wives their rights, and putting up with their character, and of bearing the harm they cause. However, there is also an element of danger here, since the man is a shepherd and thus responsible for his flock.

The third drawback lies in the possibility that a wife and children may distract him from remembering Allāh and make him spend his days and nights enjoying that. His heart might not become free to think about the Afterlife and working for it.

These are the benefits and harms of marriage. Whether it is better from a legal perspective for a person to get married or stay single goes back to his state with them. In fact, the student of the path should expose himself to the aforementioned situations and think: if the disadvantages do not apply to him and the benefits are found-meaning that he has lawful money, is well-mannered, is a youth who needs to extinguish his lust, and needs someone to arrange his house due to living alone-marriage is undoubtedly better for him. If the benefits are not there but the disadvantages apply, it is better to stay single. This applies to those who are not in need of marriage-as for those who need it, they must get married.

Section Two:
Gracious Companionship

For one to have a good marriage, the wife should have the following characteristics:

The first and most important trait is religiousness (*dīn*), for the Prophet (ﷺ) said: "Choose the one who is religious."[2] An irreligious wife will ruin her spouse's religiousness, and trouble his heart with jealous feelings, so that his life will be in turmoil

The second is good characters (*husn al-khuluq*). An ill-mannered woman brings more harm than benefit.

The third is beauty (*husn al-khalq*). This is also desirable as it is a means to chastity. This is why a man is commanded to look at the prospective wife. It is true that some men before did not care about beauty and were not after pleasure; it has been narrated, for example, that Imām Aḥmad chose a one-eyed woman instead of her sister. This, however, is rare as the nature of most men does not agree with this.

The fourth is a moderate dowry (*kiffat al-mahr*). Sa'īd Ibn al-Musayyib married off his daughter for two dirhams.

'Umar (*raḍiyAllāh 'anhu*) said: 'Do not exaggerate the dowries of women.'

And just as it is disliked for a woman to ask for a big dowry, it is equally disliked for a man to ask how much fortune she has.

[2] Muslim #715, on the authority of Jābir (*raḍiyAllah 'anhu*). A similar narration is found in the Two Ṣaḥīḥs on the authority of Abū Hurayrah (*raḍiyAllāh 'anhu*).

As [Sufyān] al-Thawrī said: 'When a man gets married and asks: 'What does the woman own?' know that he is a thief.'

The fifth is virginity (*bakkāra*): the Lawgiver has encouraged men to marry virgins. A virgin is generally more inclined and affectionate towards the man than a non-virgin (*thayyib*) which in turn creates love (*wadd*). Indeed, human beings by their very nature feel affection towards their first loves. This also makes the man love her more as men prefer that no one else has touched their women before them.

The sixth is fertility (*wulūd*).

The seventh is lineage (*nasb*): this means that a woman should be from a pious Muslim family.

The eighth is absence of close kinship (*ajnabiyya*).

This being said, just as a man should take a look at the woman, the woman's guardian should find out about the man's religiousness, character, and situation. This is because the woman becomes tied to her spouse like a slave does, so if the guardian marries her off to a sinner or an innovator, he has violated both her and himself.

A man once asked Al-Ḥasan: 'To whom should I marry my daughter?' So he replied: 'Someone who fears Allāh; if he loves her, he will honor her, and if he hates her, he will not wrong her.'

Section Three:
The Etiquette of Graceful Companionship and the Duties of Both Spouses

With respect to the husband, he has to observe moderation and good character in twelve things:

i. The wedding banquet (*walīma*): it is something recommended.

ii. Good treatment with the wives and enduring their harm which is a result of their deficient intellect. It occurs in a ṣaḥīḥ ḥadīth: "Urge yourselves to take care of women, for they were created from a rib (*dil'*). The most crooked part of a rib is above; if you try to straighten it you will break it, and if you let it be it remains crooked. So urge yourselves to take care of women."[3]

Know that good manners with a woman do not mean refraining from harming her but enduring the harm (*adha*) caused by her and showing clemency (*ḥilm*) for her heedlessness (*tais*) and (*ghadab*) anger in imitation of Allāh's Messenger (ﷺ). It occurs in the Two Ṣaḥīḥs on the authority of 'Umar (*raḍiy-Allāh 'anhu*) that the Prophet's wives once bandied words with him and one of them would stay away from him during a day until night time. This is a famous ḥadīth.[4]

iii. Playing and joking with the wife: the Prophet (ﷺ) competed with 'Ā'ishah (*raḍiy-Allāh 'anhā*)[5] and would play with his women.[6] Once, he (ﷺ) told Jābir (*raḍiy-Allāh 'anhu*): "Why did you not marry a

[3] Bukhārī, vol.5, p.217; Muslim #1468 and Tirmidhī #1188.

[4] Bukhārī, vol.9, p.278; Muslim #1479; Tirmidhī #3315; and Nasā'ī, vol.4, p.137, on the authority of 'Umar (*raḍiy-Allāh 'anhu*).

[5] Abū Dāwūd #2578; and Ibn Mājah #1979 with a sahīḥ isnād.

[6] In *al-Iḥyā'*, vol.2, p.44: "He was of those who jested with their women the most." Al-'Irāqī says: 'Al-Hasan Ibn Sufyān relates this in his *Musnad* from the ḥadīth of Anas (*raḍiy-Allāh 'anhu*) without the words: 'With their women.' It was also related by Bazzār and Ṭabarānī in *al-Saghīr* and *al-Awsaṭ*. They said: 'With a child.' Its chain includes Ibn al-Hay'a.

virgin (*bikr*) who could play with you and with whom you could play too?"[7]

iv. Not exceeding the limits of jesting by becoming so relaxed with his guardianship that the woman loses all reverence for the husband. Moderation is always good. It has been narrated that once when 'Umar Ibn al-Khaṭṭāb (*raḍiyAllāh 'anhu*) disciplined one of his employees, his wife spoke to him and asked: 'O commander of the believers, why are you upset with him?' 'Umar (*raḍiyAllāh 'anhu*) replied: "O enemy of Allāh! What do you have to do with this? You are but a toy that is played with and then left alone."[8]

v. Observing moderation (*i'tidāl*) in jealousy (*ghayra*) for the wife: This means not being unmindful of the first steps of a destructive end but not going overboard with suspicion (*ẓann*) either. Indeed, the Prophet (ﷺ) forbade one from knocking the door of his wife at night time.[9]

vi. Moderation in maintenance (*i'tidāl fi'l-nafqa wa'l-qaṣd*): one should be neither excessive (*isrāf*) nor niggardly (*taqtīr*). A man should not keep fine food from his family as that arouses bitterness.

vii. Education: Learning the rules of menstruation (*ḥayḍ*) that one needs when living with his wife. He should teach her about correct beliefs (*al-i'tiqād al-ṣaḥīḥ*) and remove any possible innovations (*bid'ah*) that she might have in her heart. He teaches her the rulings of prayer, menstruation, and chronic vaginal discharge, and tells her that if the blood stops coming before Maghrib and the time allows for

---

[7] Bukhārī, vol.9, p.104; and Muslim #715.

[8] The soundness of this is questionable. If it indeed is sound, it should be noted that his words: "*O enemy of Allāh!*" are something that the Arabs used to say frequently without actually meaning the apparent implication.

[9] Bukhārī, vol.9, p.296; Muslim #715; Abū Dāwūd #2776; Tirmidhī #1172 on the authority of Jābir (*raḍiyAllāh 'anhu*).

the performance of a single prayer unit before Maghrib begins, she has to perform both the Ẓuhr and 'Aṣr prayers[10]. If the blood stops before Fajr and the time allows for a single prayer unit before Fajr begins, she has to pray both Maghrib and 'Ishā'. This is something that most women do not realize.

viii. Equal treatment (*'adl*) with multiple wives: this pertains to sleeping with them and giving them things, not to love (*ḥubb*) and intercourse, as that is not in his hands. If he travels and wishes that one of them accompanies him, he should draw lots; whoever wins goes with him.

ix. Disciplining the rebellious wife (*nushūz*): the husband is allowed to discipline her and to obey him. However, he should proceed with this gradually by admonishing (*wa'ẓ*) and warning (*takhwīf*) her first. If this does not work, he stays away from her at night by turning his back to her or sleeping separately without speaking to her. The period of doing so should not exceed three days. If this does not work, he chastises her in a way that does not cause [any] injury, which means that he must not make her bleed or strike her face.

x. Sexual etiquette (*ādāb al-jimā'*): it is recommended to commence in Allāh's Name (*tasmiya*). One should turn away (*inḥirāf*) from the *qibla* and the couple should be under a cover without being totally naked. The husband should begin with foreplay (*mulā'iba*) by hugging (*ḍamm*) and kissing (*taqbīl*). Some scholars found it recommendable to make love on Fridays. After climax (*waṭar*), the husband should take it easy and facilitate her climax as well as it might not happen as fast as his.

[10] This is not entirely true in every case; the scholars have spoken about this in detail in the books of jurisprudence.

If the husband wishes to enjoy his wife during her menses, she must wear a waist-wrapper that covers the area between her flanks and knees. He is not allowed to have intercourse with her during that time and must never enter the anus (*dubr*). If a man wishes to make love a second time, he should wash his private part and perform ablution.

One should not shave his hair, clip his nails, or extract blood in the state of sexual impurity. With respect to coitus interruptus (*'azl*), it is permissible, though not recommended.

xi. The etiquette of having children (*ādāb al-walāda*) which includes six rules:

1. He must not be overly delighted by the birth of a boy nor grief when a girl is born; he does not know which one is better.

2. He should perform the *adhan* into the newborn's ear after birth.

3. He should give him a fine name. It occurs in the collection of Muslim: "The most beloved of your names to Allāh are 'Abdullāh and 'Abdu'l-Raḥmān."[11]

If one has a name that is disliked, he is encouraged to change it, for the Prophet changed the names of a number of people.[12]

Disliked names include Aflaḥ, Nāfi', Yasār, Rabāḥ, and Baraka, for people may ask: "Does this person really have this attribute?" and

[11] Muslim #2132; Tirmidhī #2835; and Abū Dāwūd #4949 on the authority of Ibn 'Umar (*raḍiy Allāh 'anhumā*).
[12] Refer to *Jāmi' al-Uṣūl*, vol.1, p.371, Chapter Three: "Those Whose Names Were Changed by the Prophet."

the reply might be no.[13]

4. *'Aqīqah*: He should sacrifice two sheep for a boy and one for a girl.

5. *al-Taḥnīq*: He should rub the palate of the child with a date or a sweet.

6. *Al-Khattān*: He should circumcise the child.

xii. Divorce (*ṭalāq*) is permissible, but it is the most hateful to Allāh (ﷻ) of all permissible things[15]. It is disliked for a man to suddenly divorce his wife with no prior discrimination on her part. Neither is a woman allowed to force his hand and make him divorce her. If it so happens that he wants divorce, he should observe four things[16]:

1. He must divorce her after her menses when he has not yet had intercourse with her. In this way, her waiting period will not be long.

2. He should only divorce her to a single [repudiation pronouncement] so that he can take her back (*rij'a*) if he regrets (*nadm*) it.

3. He should handle the issue with kindness by giving the grieving woman what soothes her. Indeed, it has been narrated that when

---

[13] Muslim #2138; Abū Dāwūd #4960 on the authority of Samura Ibn Jundub (*raḍiy Allāh 'anhu*).

[14] For details on everything that has thus far been mentioned, refer to *Tuḥfat al-Mawlūd* by Ibn al-Qayyim.

[15] The ḥadīth: "The most hated permissible thing by Allāh is divorce" is weak. It was related by Abū Dāwūd #2178; and al-Bayhaqī, vol.7, p.322 on the authority of Ibn 'Umar (*raḍiy Allāh 'anhu*). The erudite scholar al-Albānī presented a completely sufficient criticism of this ḥadīth in *Irwā' al-Ghalīl* #2040.

16 For further detail on these and their academic evidences, refer to *al-Isti'nās li Tashīḥ Ankihat al-Nās* by al-Qāsimī with my checking (Dar 'Ammar li al-Nashr wa al-Tawzī', Amman, 1985).

Al-Ḥasan Ibn 'Alī (*raḍiyAllāh 'anhumā*) divorced a woman, he sent ten thousand dirhams to her after whom she said: "Small enjoyment from a beloved that has left."

4. He must not spread her secrets (*sirr*): it occurs in the collection of Muslim: "One of the worst people in status before Allāh on the Day of Resurrection is a man who goes to his wife while she too goes to him and then spreads her secrets."[17]

It is narrated that one of the pious once wanted to divorce his wife. When he was asked: 'What makes you dislike her?' he said: 'An intelligent person does not reveal a secret.' When he had divorced her he was asked: 'What made you divorce her?' His reply was: 'I do not wish to talk about a woman that is not mine.'

All that has been mentioned pertains to the duties of the husband. The second category of gracious companionship pertains to those of the wife:

Abū Umāmah (*raḍiyAllāh 'anhu*) narrates that he heard Allāh's Messenger (ﷺ) say: "Were it allowed for someone to prostrate to someone, I would order women to prostrate to their husbands."[18] This is due to her tremendous duty towards her husband. There are numerous traditions that emphasize the husband's rights over his wife. These rights are many, but the most important are two: The first is concealment (*sitr*) and protection (*ṣiyāna*), and the second is contentment (*qanā'a*).

[17] Muslim #1437; Abū Dāwūd #4870; Aḥmad, vol.3, p.69, on the authority of Abū Sa'eed al-Khudrī (*raḍiyAllāh 'anhu*).

[18] Tirmidhī #1159 on the authority of Abū Hurayrah (*raḍiyAllāh 'anhu*); Abū Dāwūd #2140 on the authority of Qays Ibn Sa'd (*raḍiyAllāh 'anhu*). A ḥadīth on the topic has also narrated from Mu'adh, 'Ā'ishah, Anas, Ibn 'Umar (*raḍiyAllāh 'anhum*), and others. It is ṣaḥīḥ.

This was the way of the women in the time of the predecessors (*salaf*). When a man would leave his home his wife would tell him: "Beware of unlawful earnings, for we can endure hunger but cannot endure the fire."

She must not behave neglectfully with his property (*māl*). If she feeds others by his consent, she gets the same reward as he does, but if she does so without his permission, he gets the reward (*ajr*) and she gets the sin (*wizr*).

Her parents should discipline her before marrying her off so that she might know how to live with her husband. A woman should sit at home and stay with her spindle. She should not talk much with the neighbours and should stay away from people a lot when her husband is absent. She must protect him in his presence and absence and seeks to make him happy at all times. She does not betray him when it comes to herself or when it comes to his property and must not let anyone he dislikes set foot in the house nor anyone else either without his permission. Let her worry about her own condition and taking care of the household by serving the home to the best of her ability. She should put her husband's rights before her own rights and the rights of all her relatives.

Chapter Three

On the Ethics in Earning a Livelihood

Know that in His gentleness and wisdom, Allāh Exalted and Most High has made this world a place of utilizing means and earning (*iktisāb*)-sometimes to make a living (*ma'āsh*) and sometimes for the Afterlife. We shall now explain the ethics of commerce (*tijārāt*) and trade (*sinā'āt*), the necessity of having an income, and how one should make his earnings.

Section One:
On the Virtues of Work and Exhortation Towards It

Allāh says:

وَجَعَلْنَا ٱلنَّهَارَ مَعَاشًا ﴿١١﴾

"And We have made the day for livelihood."

[*al-Nabā'* (78): 11]

and He mentioned this in the context of exhibiting His blessings [on humankind]. And He Most High says:

وَجَعَلْنَا لَكُمْ فِيهَا مَعَايِشَ قَلِيلًا مَّا تَشْكُرُونَ ﴿١٠﴾

"And We have established you on earth and provided you a means of livelihood thereon. Little are you grateful."
[*al-A'rāf* (7): 10]

Thus He has made livelihood a blessing and demanded gratitude for it. And He Most High says:

لَيْسَ عَلَيْكُمْ جُنَاحٌ أَن تَبْتَغُوا فَضْلًا مِّن رَّبِّكُمْ

"It is no crime for you to seek bounty from your Lord."
[*al-Baqarah* (2):198]

It occurs in a ḥadīth that the Prophet (ﷺ) said: "Seeking for the lawful is exertion (*jihād*)."[1]

and: "Verily, Allāh loves a servant with a profession (*al-'abd al-muḥtarif*)."[2]

In a ḥadīth in the collection of Bukhārī the Prophet (ﷺ) says: "No one has ever eaten better food than that which he has earned with his own hands. Indeed, Allāh's Prophet Dāwūd (*'alayhis-salām*) used to eat from the earnings of his own hands."[3]

In another ḥadīth he says: "Prophet Zakariyah (*'alayhis-salām*) was

[1] Al-Qudā'ī: *al-Musnad* #82 from Ibn 'Abbās (*raḍiy-Allah 'anhu*); Abū 'Abdu'l-Rahmān al-Sulamī: *Tabaqat al-Sufiyya*, p. 281; Abū Nu'aym: *al-Hilyah* on the authority of Ibn 'Umar (*raḍiy-Allāh 'anhu*). It includes Muḥammad Ibn Marwān al-Suddī. Al-Dhahabī relates it in *al-Mīzān*, vol.4, p.33, and says: 'They left him.' Then he related this hadith of his as one of his disclaimed reports. Refer also to: *Fayd al-Qadīr*, vol.4, p.270.

[2] Ibn 'Adī, vol.1, p.369; and Tabarānī: *al-Kabīr* #13200. It includes Ash'ath Ibn Abī Sa'īd al-Sammān who is extremely weak. Al-Dhahabī relates it in *al-Mīzān*, vol.1, p.263, as one of his disclaimed reports. Refer also to: *Majma' al-Zawa'id*, vol.4, p.26.

[3] Bukhārī, vol.4, p.259 on the authority of al-Miqdām (*raḍiy-Allāh 'anhu*).

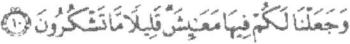

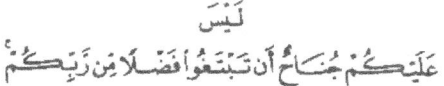

a carpenter."[4]

Ibn 'Abbās (*radiy-Allāh 'anhu*) says: "Ādam (*'alayhis-salām*) was a cultivator, Nūḥ (*'alayhis-salām*) was a carpenter, Idrīs (*'alayhis-salām*) was a tailor, Ibrāhīm (*'alayhis-salām*) and Lūṭ (*'alayhis-salām*) were farmers, Ṣāliḥ (*'alayhis-salām*) was a merchant, Dāwūd (*'alayhis-salām*) was an armor manufacturer, and Mūsā (*'alayhis-salām*), Shu'ayb (*'alayhis-salām*), and Muḥammad (ﷺ), were shepherds."

As was other reports, it has been narrated that Luqmān al-Ḥakīm said to his son: 'O my son, seek independence from poverty through lawful earning, for indeed, not a single person becomes impoverished except that he is afflicted by three traits: vulnerability in his religion, weakness in his intelligence, and loss of his dignity. And what is greater than these three is people's belittling of him.'

Aḥmad Ibn Ḥanbal was once asked: 'What do you say about a man who sits in his house or in the masjid and says: 'I will not do anything; my provisions will come to me'? Aḥmad replied: 'This is a man who lacks knowledge. Has he not heard the Prophet's (ﷺ) words: "Allāh has placed my provisions (*rizq*) in the shade of my spear?"[5] When birds were mentioned, he (ﷺ) said: "They go in the morning while hungry and come back in the evening with a full stomach."[6]

Indeed, the Companions of Allāh's Messenger (ﷺ) used to do trade on both land and sea and work on their palm trees, and they are the ones we should follow.

Abū Sulaymān al-Darānī said: 'Worship in our view does not mean

[4] Muslim #2379; and Ibn Mājah #2150 on the authority of Abū Hurayrah (*radiy-Allāh 'anhu*).
[5] Ahmad, vol.2, p.50, 92; and al-Ṭahāwi, *Mushkil al-Āthar*, vol.1, p.88 on the authority of Ibn 'Umar (*radiy-Allāh 'anhuma*). Al-Albānī declared it ṣaḥīḥ in *al-Irwa'* #1269.
[6] Ahmad, vol.1, p.30; Tirmidhī #2345; Ḥākim, vol.4, p.318 on the authority of 'Umar with a ṣaḥīḥ isnād.

that you stand with your feed side by side (i.e. that you are praying) while someone else tires himself for you. Begin with your two pieces of bread and ensure their existence-then devote yourself to worship.'

If it is now said that Abu'l-Dardā' (*radiy-Allāh 'anhu*) stated: 'I pursued both trade and worship (*'ibādah*). They could not be combined, so I chose worship.' The answer to this is that trade is not the goal-being independent, providing enough for the family, and being gracious towards one's brother is. If one makes amassing wealth, boasting (*tafākur*) with it, and other such things the actual goal, then that is censured (*madhmūm*).

It behooves that the contractual agreement (*al-'aqd*) by which this earning is realized fulfills four conditions: validity (*al-ṣiḥḥa*), justice (*al-'adl*), benevolence (*al-iḥsān*), and concern (*al-shafaqa*) for the religion.

The First: On the Science of Valid Selling, Buying and Transactions

If the transaction is selling (*al-bay'*), its three pillars must be observed: the contracting parties, the merchandise, and the wording.

1. With respect to the contracting parties, a merchant should not do trade with an insane person (*majnūn*) because he is not legally responsible (*mukhallaf*) and as such his buying and selling are not valid. He should neither do business with a slave unless he knows that he has been given the permission to buy. The same applies to children: he must not sell anything to them unless their fathers or guardians have allowed it, in which case the ruling of a slave with permission applies to them. Al-Shāfi'ī was of the opinion that the transactions of a child are not legally binding whatever the case. As

for the transactions of a blind person, we consider them valid, so his buying and selling are legally binding. Al-Shāfiʿī, however, did not hold this opinion.

With respect to oppressors and people whose wealth is mostly unlawful (*ḥarām*), trade with them should be practiced only when it is known that the wealth they are offering is lawful (*ḥalāl*).

2. With respect to the merchandise, which is the property being traded, it should be known that selling dogs is impermissible due to their impurity. As for mules and donkeys, they can be sold whether one hold that they are pure or not. Selling insects is unlawful as is selling musical reeds, lutes, clay images, and other such things. It is also impermissible to sell something that one cannot actually deliver or is not allowed to deliver in the Islāmic law. An example of what one cannot actually deliver would be a bird in the sky or a runaway slave, and an example of what one is not allowed to deliver in the law would be selling collateral or a mother without her small child or vice versa. It is unlawful to deliver things of this sort.

3. With respect to the wording, it must contain an offer (*ijāb*) and its acceptance (*qabūl*). If acceptance is uttered before the offer, the transaction is invalid according to one of the two reports (from Aḥmad) and valid according to the other. The ruling applies whether the wording is in past tense or in the form of a command. If a transaction is conducted without words, the apparent implication of Aḥmad's statements is that the transaction is valid.

Qāḍī Abū Yaʿlā, however, says that such transactions are only valid in small things, and this-that wordless trade should only take place with merchandise of little value-is the most solid opinion because the people are accustomed to it. Cautiousness should still be observed, however, by not omitting the offer and acceptance. By taking the more cautious opinion, one avoids what is doubtful (*shubah*).

Allāh Most High has given a severe warning about usury, so one must beware of it. Usury is of two types: usury of excess (*ribā al-faḍl*) and usury of delay (*ribā al-nasi'a*). He must know this and must know what things the rules of usury (*al-ribā*) apply to. He also needs to know the conditions of buying in advance (*al-salam*), hiring and renting (*al-ijāra*), business partnership (*al-sharika*), for all business transactions revolve around these contracts.

The Second:

On the Exposition of Justice (*al-'adl*) in Transactions, Avoiding Oppression and the Prohibition of Hoarding

What we mean here with mistreatment is doing something that harms others. This harm is either something that extends to everyone or something that is restricted to specific people:

1. What harms people in general: hoarding (*dhakira*). This is impermissible as it leads to high prices and keeps foodstuffs (*al-aqwāt*) from people. What is meant with hording is purchasing a lot of produce with the intention of raising the prices. This does not apply to withholding the produce of one's own land. Neither is one consider a hoarder if he buys produce in times of abundance and ease without causing difficulty to the people. In general, doing trade with food (*qūt*) is disliked because human need it to survive.

2. What harms specific people: things like unnecessary praise of the merchandise or concealment of some of its faults, thereby harming the consumer. The Prophet (ﷺ) said: "He who cheats us is not one of us."*

* Muslim #101; Tirmidhī #1315; Abū Dāwūd #3452; Ibn Mājah #2224 on the authority of Abū Hurayrah (*raḍiy-Allāh 'anhu*).

Know that cheating (*gishsh*) is unlawful in both trade and manufacture (*ṣinā'āt*). When Imām Aḥmad was asked about mending a garment so that the rent is not visible he said: 'One is not allowed to conceal it if he sells it.'

A merchant should weigh accurately, and to ensure this, he should give more and take less. If a seller of provender mixes soil with it before measuring it, he is a guilty of scantiness, and so if a butcher who mixes with the meat bones that normally are not there.

Also forbidden is offering an unusually high price for something without intending to buy it in order to deceive another consumer[8] and not milking a camel for many days to make the consumers think it produces a lot of milk.

The Third: On the Exposition of benevolence (*al-iḥsān*) in Transactions

Allāh Most High has commanded us to observe justice (*'adl*) and benevolence (*iḥsān*) together, and one form of benevolence is that which takes place in buying and selling. One should not bargain for more than what the people are accustomed to. This is not to say that bargaining is not allowed as the purpose of selling is making profit (*al-ribḥ*), but one must be moderate. If a consumer really wants the merchandise and pays more than what the people are accustomed to, the merchant should refuse to accept it. This is a form of benevolence.

If a merchant want to collect the entire price (*thaman*) of the mer-

[8] Bukhārī, vol.4, p.298; Muslim #1516; Mālik, vol.2, p.684; Nasā'ī, vol.7, p.258; and Ibn Mājah #2173 on the authority of Ibn 'Umar (*raḍiy Allāh 'anhumā*).

chandise or a debt (*dain*) from a consumer, it is commendable to waive it completely, decrease it, grant respite (*musāmaḥa*), be lenient (*tasāhul*), or not demand high quality.

If a consumer seeks the abrogation of a sale, the merchant should be kind and abrogate it, for a person only desires to abrogate a sale due to some harm. There are traditions that mention the virtue (*faḍl*) and reward (*thawāb*) of what has preceded.

The fourth:

On the Merchant's Concern for His Religion

A merchant should be compassionate (*shafqa*) towards what pertains to his Afterlife. Therefore, he must not let his earnings distract him from the Afterlife and must take care of his religious duties. This compassion can only be completed by observing six things:

1. A good intention (*ḥusn al-niyya*) when doing trade: he should aim for self-sufficiency where he does not need to ask others and hope for their help. He should also intend to be able to take care of his family and thereby become one of those who struggle in Allāh's path. He should discharge the [the duty of] giving good counsel to Muslims (nusḥ lil-Muslimeen).

2. He should manufacture or trade with the intention of performing a communal obligation. After all, if manufacture or trade would be abandoned people would not be able to live. This being said, there are types of manufacture that are important and types that are not necessary as they only produce beauty or pleasure. A manufacturer should therefore focus on something important and cover a significant task for the Muslims. Let him avoid molding, carving, and cementing buildings with gypsum and decorating them, for all of that is disliked.

It is sinful for a tailor to make a *qabā'*[9] from silk brocade for a man. It is disliked to be a butcher as it hardens the heart (*qasāwat al-qalb*), or a cupper or a cleaner as that entails direct contact with filth (*najāsa*). The same applies to a tanner.

It is impermissible to collect a price (*ajarah*) for teaching the Qur'ān or teaching about acts of worship (*'ibadāt*) and communal obligations (*farūḍ al-qafāyāt*). [Scholars have different views regarding this, it is permissible to have a reasonable charge for teaching the Qur'ān. And Allāh knows best.]

3. He should not let the commerce of this world prevent him from the commerce of the Afterlife which is in the masjid. Therefore, one should schedule the first part of the day for his Afterlife before going to the market and be consistent in observing his litanies (*awrād*). Indeed, the pious merchant of our predecessors used to schedule the first and last parts of the day for the Afterlife and did commerce in the middle. Then, when one hears the adhan of Ẓuhr and 'Aṣr, he must leave his commerce and occupy himself with the current obligation.

4. He should remember Allāh Most High at the market constantly, reciting *tasbih "subḥānAllāh"* and *tahlīl "lā ilāha illAllāh."*

5. He should not be extremely eager (*shadīd al-ḥirṣ*) to attend the market and do commerce. Therefore, let him not be the first to enter the marketplace and the last to leave.

6. He must not only avoid the unlawful (*ḥarām*) but should also avoid everything that is doubtful (*shubah*). He should not just follow the legal verdicts (*fatāwā*) that are out there but should consult his heart if something causes it to waver.

[9] *Qabā'* is a garment that is worn above the clothes or a garment that is wound around the body.

Chapter Four

On the Ethics in the Lawful and the Unlawful

Know that seeking the lawful (*halāl*) is obligatory (*fard*) on every Muslim. Many ignoramuses have claimed that nothing is lawful anymore save sweet water and grass that grows on the ground. Besides that-according to them-everything else has been ruined by invalid transactions. When people started to think like this while realizing that they have to eat, they indulged in the doubtful (*shubha*) and unlawful (*harām*). This is a result of ignorance (*jahl*) and lack of knowledge (*qila al-'ilm*), for it occurs in the Two Ṣaḥīḥs from al-Nu'mān Ibn Basheīr (*raḍiy Allāh 'anhu*) that the Prophet (ﷺ) said: "The lawful is clear and the unlawful is clear, and between them are matters that are doubtful."[1]

Due to the fact that the claim of these ignoramuses is an innovation (*bid'ah*) of widespread harm and evil that has been mixed with the religion, its corrupt reality must be exposed by showing the people

[1] Bukhārī, vol.1, pp117; Muslim #1599; Abū Dāwūd #3329; and Nasā'ī, vol.7, pp 241.

how to distinguish the lawful, unlawful, and doubtful from each other. We shall clarify this in the following categories:

The first category: The excellence of seeking the lawful, and the reprehensibility of the unlawful, and the degrees of the lawful and the unlawful

Allāh [Exalted is He] has said:

يَٰٓأَيُّهَا ٱلرُّسُلُ كُلُوا۟ مِنَ ٱلطَّيِّبَٰتِ وَٱعْمَلُوا۟ صَٰلِحًا

"O Messengers, partake of the good things and work righteousness."

[*al-Mu'minūn* (23):51]

The meaning of '*good things*' (*ṭayyibāt*) is the lawful, and He gave the command to consume good things before he commanded the working of righteousness. In rebuke of the unlawful He has said:

وَلَا تَأْكُلُوٓا۟ أَمْوَٰلَكُم بَيْنَكُم بِٱلْبَٰطِلِ

"And do not consume one another's wealth unjustly."

[*al-Baqarah* (2):188]

There are also other verses to this effect.

Abū Hurayrah (*raḍiyAllāh 'anhu*) narrates that Allāh's Messenger (ﷺ) said: "People! Allāh is good (*ṭayyib*) and accepts only good (*ṭayyib*)." Then he related the ḥadīth and said: "Then he mentioned a man who has travelled long; his hair is shaggy and his body is dusty as he raises his hands towards the sky and says: 'My Lord! My Lord!' But his food is unlawful, his drink is unlawful, and his clothes are unlawful. He has been nourished by the unlawful. So how can that be answered?"[2] There are numerous traditions about this.

[2] Muslim #1015; and Tirmidhī #2992.

It has been narrated that Sa'īd (*raḍiy-Allāh 'anhu*) once requested Allāh's Messenger (ﷺ) to have his supplication answered so he told him: "Make your food good and your supplication will be answered."[3]

Indeed, the predecessors would scrutinize food in search for the lawful so much so that once when Abū Bakr al-Ṣiddīq (*raḍiy-Allāh 'anhu*) ate something doubtful, he vomited it.[4]

Section One:

Exposition on the degrees of the Lawful and the Unlawful

Know that what is lawful, all of it, is good (*ṭayyib*); but some of it is better than others, and likewise what is unlawful, all of it, is iniquitous (*kabīth*), but some of it is more iniquitous than others. This can be compared to a doctor who says that all sweet things are 'hot', but continues to state that this particular type are hotter than others, and this one comes after that, and this third one comes after that, and this one here is the less pungent of them all. An example of this is acquiring something through an invalid contract: it is unlawful but not on the level of seizing something by force. The latter is graver as it entails harming others and neglecting the prescribed way of acquiring things while an invalid contract is but negligence of correct worship. Similarly, wrongful seizure from a poor or righteous man is graver than taking the property of a strong, wealthy, or sinful person.

[3] Al-'Irāqī says in *Takhrij al-Iḥyā'*, vol.2, pp 89: Ṭabarānī related it in *al-Awsaṭ*: 'Its chain includes narrators I do not know.'

[4] Because it was bought with the impure earnings of a fortuneteller.

Section Two:
Exposition on the degrees of Prudence

There are four degrees of prudence (*wara'*):

1. The first degree: The Prudence of the Upright (*wara' al-'adūl*) is prudence in regard to all that may be prohibited unlawful by means of legal edicts (*fatāwa*) and there is no need to give examples.

2. The second degree: [The Prudence of the Pious] includes, avoiding everything dubious thing that one is only encouraged but not obliged to avoid. This will be explained in the chapter on '*The Degrees of the Dubious*'. It is to this degree that the Prophet (ﷺ) said: "Forsake what makes you doubtful in favour of what does not make you doubtful."[5]

3. The third degree: [The Prudence of the Heedful] includes, avoiding some lawful things in fear of falling into the unlawful.

4. The fourth degree: This includes, avoiding everything that is not for Allāh. This is the Prudence of the Truthful (*wara' al-Siddīqīn*). For example, it has been related concerning Yaḥyā Ibn Yaḥyā al-Naysabūrī that one day he drank medicine, and his wife told him: 'Walk a little in the house so that the medicine will begin to affect.' He replied: 'I do not know a walking like this, and I have taken myself into account for thirty years.'

This is a man who did not walk because he did not find himself having a religious intention in doing so. This is an example of very delicate and subtle prudence.

[5] Tirmidhī #2525; Nasā'ī, vol.8, pp.327 from Al-Ḥasan Ibn 'Alī (*raḍiy Allāh 'anhuma*) with a sound chain. A ḥadīth on the topic has also been narrated by Ibn Mas'ūd (*raḍiy Allāh 'anhu*).

The truth of this matter is that prudence has a beginning (*awwal*) and an end (*ghāya*) and between them are several degrees of prudence. The stricter one is with oneself, the quicker he passes over the bridge [on the Day of Judgement] and the lighter his burden is. The stations (*manāzil*) in the Afterlife will differ on the basis of the different degrees (*darajāt*) of prudence exercised in this world. Likewise, the stations of Hell will differ for tyrants on the basis of the different degrees of the unlawful [they committed or consumed]. So if you like, increase your prudence, and if you wish, take dispensations-you are only being cautious for your own sake and your dispensations harm none but you.

The second category: The degrees of the dubious (*marātib al-shubahāt*) and how to distinguish them from the lawful and unlawful. The ḥadīth of al-Nuʿmān Ibn Bashīr[6] mentions these three, meaning the lawful, the unlawful, and what is between them. What needs clarification is what lies in the middle and what many people have no knowledge of. These are the doubtful matters.

Thus, we however, shed light on this now and say what follows: What is *'strictly lawful'* (*al-ḥalāl al-mutlaq*) is that which there are no intrinsic attributes that make it unlawful in and of itself, and in which there are no extrinsic reasons for it to be unlawful (*taḥrīm*) or disliked (*karaha*).

An example of this would be rainwater that one takes before it falls on anyone's property.

What is *'strictly unlawful'* (*al-ḥarām al-mahd*) is that in which there is an undoubted attribute of the unlawful; like the intoxicating of wine and the impure in urine, or in such an attributes came to be through unlawful means like oppression (*zulm*), or usury (*ribā*).

[6] The source of this ḥadīth has been mentioned earlier.

These are the two self-evident opposite. The same also applies to things that are clear like them but might change due to factors that are not clear. For example, the game taken on land and from the sea is lawful, but when one catches a gazelle or fish there is always a theoretical chance that they are the escaped property of another hunter. Such a possibility does not apply to rainwater that is gathered from the air. Thinking like this, however, is nothing but *'the cautious of the Overly Suspicious'* (*wara' al-muwaswisīn*). These are but baseless assumptions. Real cautiousness is observed when there is an actual sign like a wound but one is not sure whether it is something that can only be inflicted after capturing it, as it the case with cauterization, for example, or a normal wound.

As for the definition of a doubtful matter, it is anything regarding which there are two contradictory beliefs, both caused by something. There are many examples of such scenarios, but the most important are two:

1. Reasonable doubt (*shakk*) about what made something lawful or unlawful: this has four categories:

The first category: When the unlawful is known beforehand, and then doubts whether it has become lawful or not. Such kind of doubt must be avoided and is unlawful to act upon. For example, a hunter might see an animal and wound it so that it falls into the water, and then after reaching it finds that it has died. If he does not know whether it drowned or died by the wound, eating it is unlawful. The reason for this is that the legal presumption (*aṣl*) will always be for prohibition (*taḥrīm*).

The second category: When there is doubt concerning an unlawful factor in something known to be lawful. The legal presumption in such matters is that they are lawful [unless there is a proof to the contrary]. For example, two men upon seeing a bird fly overhead, one of the men says: 'If that is a crow, my wife is divorced!' Then the other man says: 'If that is not a crow, my wife is divorced!' If the matter does not become clear, we do not declare the wife of either one as divorced. Prudence, however, dictates that both should divorce their wives and stay away from them.

The third category: When something is unlawful but then some factor most likely necessitates its lawfulness and thus renders it questionable. Then the preferred ruling is that it is lawful. An example of this is when one shoots game that then runs out of sight and is later found dead with no other sign [as to the cause of death] then the hunter's arrow, if an animal runs out of sight after a hunter has shot it and he then finds it dead with no other marks on it save his arrow, the obvious ruling is that the animal is lawful. This is due to the fact that if a possibility is not based on any evidence, entertaining it is considered unfounded suspicion (*waswās*). If, however, the animal shows signs of being struck or wounded by something else, it takes the ruling of the first category.

The fourth category: When something is known to be lawful but then considers it very likely that something that has weight in the law has rendered it unlawful. For example, one may believe that one of two vessels is impure based on a sign that necessitates the strong likelihood of that. As a result, it is unlawful for him to drink this water or use for ablution. Another example could be something lawful and unlawful becoming mixed up so that one is not sure which one is which.

This includes different types of scenarios:

The first type of intermixture is when an animal that has died without legal slaughter is mixed up with a legally slaughtered one, with ten legally slaughtered ones, or with any other number of them. Or when [a nursed] sister is mixed with unrelated (*ajnabiyya*) women. It is obligatory to avoid doubtful things of this sort.

The second type of intermixture is when a limited quantity of something unlawful is mixed up with an unlimited quantity of something lawful. This would be like a nursed sister, or even ten of them, intermixing in a big city. Such circumstances would not mean that he [without knowing exactly who they were] would have to refrain from marrying in that city. On the contrary, he may marry whosoever he desires to marry because declaring all of them unlawful would entail great hardship. Similarly, no one has any doubt that some of the money in this world is unlawful, yet we are not obliged to refrain from buying things and eating them. This is because a ruling like that would entail hardship. The Messenger of Allāh (ﷺ) and his Companions were well aware that some people deal with usury, yet they did not stop using dirhams completely. They also knew that a shield was stolen in his time[7], but that did not make them stop buying shields. Therefore, such abstinence is no more than *'the prudence of the overly suspicious'* (*wara' al- waswasa*)!

The third type of intermixture is when an unlimited quantity of something unlawful is mixed up with an unlimited quantity of something lawful like the money of our times[8]. This does not mean that taking something of those things is unlawful unless something indicates that the very portion that one is taking is a part of the unlawful. An example of this would be taking money from the hand of a despotic ruler: if there is no sign, it is cautious to refrain but taking it is not unlawful. It was known in the time of the Messenger of Allāh (ﷺ) as well as in the time of the Rightly-Guided Caliphs after

[7] Bukhārī #6792; Muslim #1686; Mālik, vol.2, pp.832; Tirmidhī #1445; Abū Dāwūd #4383; and Nasā'ī, vol.8, pp.77 from 'Ā'ishah (*radiy-Allāh 'anha*).
[8] So what about our time?!

him, money in exchange for wine or invested usurious transactions or misappropriated from the spoils of war, was intermixed with all other money. The Companions also witnessed to see tyrannical rulers and when the city of Medina was pillaged, but did not stop people from buying and selling in the marketplace [when it reopened]. Were these transactions invalid, the door to every single type of transaction would be sealed, for most people are of the sinful type.

The default ruling of wealth is lawfulness, and if a default ruling and what is common conflict and there is no sign to support what is common, precedence is given to the default ruling. This is what we have said earlier regarding dust in the streets and the vessels of the polytheists.

Indeed, 'Umar (*raḍiy-Allāh 'anhu*) performed ablution from the vessels of the Christian, even though they were known to drink wine and consume the flesh of swine and were not cautious with impurities, and the Companions used to wear tanned skins and dyed garments. If one thinks about what the tanners and dyers do, he knows that they are covered with impurities. This indicates clearly that they were only cautious with impurities they could see or filth that was known to exist due to a sign. As for suspicion (*ẓann*) and conjecture (*wahm*) based on the circumstances (*aḥwāl*), they did not pay attention to it.

Someone might now say: 'The Companions are known to have been very particular in matters of purity (*tahāra*) as they avoided everything that might have been unlawful, so what is the difference?' To this we answer by saying that if you mean that they used to pray with impurity on them, you are wrong, but if you mean that they used to avoid all impurities that had to be avoided, you are right. As for their avoidance of doubtful matters, it was about avoiding things that were allowable in fear of things that were not. The soul is inclined towards wealth no matter what form it takes but this is not the case with impurity. The Companions used refrain from the lawful things that occupied their hearts. And Allāh knows best.

The third category: When one should look into the lawfulness of something and inquire about it

Know that if food is brought to you, or someone gives you a gift, or you want to buy something from someone, you are not allowed to say: 'I am not sure about its lawfulness and need to investigate (*baḥth*) the matter.' That said, you are not allowed to completely refrain from looking into the matter either. Rather, it is sometimes essential that you question (*su'āl*), and sometimes it is obligatory (*farḍ*), and sometimes it is prohibited (*ḥarām*), and sometimes it is recommended (*mandūb*), and sometimes it is disproved (*makrūh*).

A satisfactory explanation of this is as follows: what entitles one to ask is doubt, and doubt occurs due to something in the wealth or the owner of the wealth.

For example, if the owner is unknown due to not bearing any signs of a wrongdoer, like military clothing, or of a pious man, like the garments of the scholars and ascetics, one is not obliged to question him anything. In fact, questioning him is not permissible as that entails degradation and harming of another Muslim. Wealth like this is not called questionable, for a thing is only defined as questionable when doubt concerning it occurs due to evidence. Such evidence could be the man looking like a Turk[9], or one of the Bedouins known for their oppression (*ẓulm*), or a highway-robber. Even then it is permissible to deal with him because the fact that he has the property indicates that he owns it and the aforementioned signs are not strong evidence.

[9] Meaning one of their soldiers. This was the case in the author's time as pointed out by al-Zabidī in *Sharḥ al-Iḥyā'*, vol.6, pp.81.

However, it is praiseworthy prudence to abstain dealing with him.

With respect to doubt regarding the capital itself, it could happen, for example, that lawful things get intermixed with unlawful ones. If stolen food arrives at the market-place and the merchants buy it, the buyers of that market-place in that town are not obliged to ask about the food they purchase. Asking becomes necessary only when it is likely that most of what they offer is unlawful, but if this is not the case, it will be prudent to investigate (*taftīsh*) but not necessary (*wājib*).

The same is said about a man who has lawful and unlawful money. He might be, for example, a merchant whose business is generally valid but he deals with usury. If majority of his money is unlawful, it is not permissible to answer his invitation or gifts before investigating into the matter. If one then finds out that what is being offered came from a lawful source, he is allowed to accept it, and if not, he must refrain. If the unlawful money is less, what is being offered is regarded as doubtful (*shubha*) and a prudent person avoids it.

Know that one only asks due to suspicion (*rība*), so questioning does not end until the reason to doubt (*rība*) is no longer there. This means that the one being asked should not be a suspicious person. If he is suspicious and you know that he has an ulterior motive in inviting you or giving you a gift, you must not trust his words. Instead, you should ask someone else.

The fourth category: How the repentant compensates for financial iniquity.

Know that anyone who repents while in possession of wealth of which a portion is known to have been unlawfully obtained, he is obliged to segregate and extract what is unlawful from the lawful. If the amount is known, then matter is easy, but if he cannot distinguish it from the rest, he should look: if the unlawful and the lawful are the same sort, such as when everything is crops, money, or oils, and the amount is known, he takes away that amount. If the matter proves difficult, he has two options:

One is to take out what he thinks is most likely correct and the other is to take out enough to leave no room for doubt.

After segregating the unlawful property, he must return it to the owner or his heirs if the owner is known. If that specific property has increased in amount or benefit, he gathers all of it and gives it to the rightful owner. If he has no hope of finding the owner and does not know whether he has died or not and whether he has left any heirs, he should give the property in charity. If the money was taken from the spoils of *Fay'* and the money put aside to benefit the Muslims, he should spend it on the construction of bridges and masjids and the development of the road of Makkah in any way that benefits the Muslim travelers.

Issue: If a person has both lawful and doubtful money, he should use the lawful money for himself. He should consider his food and clothing first before things like the cupper's fee, oil, and heating the oven. This is because the Prophet (ﷺ) said about the earnings of a cupper (*hajjām*): "Feed your camel with it."[10]

If the earnings of one's parents are unlawful, he should refrain from eating with them. If their money is doubtful, he should advise them gently. If they do not accept his advice, he should only take a little.

Indeed, it has been narrated that the mother of Bishr al-Ḥāfī once

[10] Tirmidhī #1277; Abū Dāwūd #3422; Ibn Mājah #2166; al-Baghawī #2034; and Aḥmad, vol.5, pp.436 from Muhayyisa with a ṣaḥīḥ isnād.

gave him a date and he ate it, but after that he went up to the room and vomited it.

The fifth category: Grants and gifts made by the rulers and sultans, having close ties with them, and the permissible ways of accompanying oppressive rulers.

Know that before accepting a gift from the ruler, he must consider how that gift came to be in the possession of the ruler in the first place, one has to find out where the Sultan got it from, whether it is of the type that can be taken, and whether he is deserving of the amount offered. Some (of the pious) used to practice prudence and avoided it while others accepted it and then gave it away as charity (*ṣadaqa*).

As for these times, it is best to stay away from it because the way the money has been acquired is known and it can only be received by humiliation (*dull*), asking (*su'āl*), and refraining from criticism (*sukūt 'alā inkār*).

One of the predecessors refused to take it on the basis that others who also deserved it had not taken it, but this is not right at all. Had he taken it, he would have only taken what was rightfully his in spite of the fact that the rest would have remained in their position of those who were wronged (*maqām al-maẓlūm*). That money was not the common property of them all.

Section Three:

Exposition on the State of those who Socialise with Tyrannical Rulers

Know that your state with tyrannical rulers and officials is one of the three:

First, that you visit them and this is the worst state, for it has been narrated that the Prophet (ﷺ) said: "Whoever goes to the gates of the rulers will be tried. A servant never gets closer to the ruler but he also gets further from Allāh."[11]

Hudhayfah (*raḍiy-Allāh 'anhu*) said: 'Beware of the places of tribulation!' He was asked: 'And what are they?' Hudhayfah replied: 'The doors of the rulers. One of you may visit the ruler and find yourself verifying his untruths, and saying things about him that are not true.'

Some of the rulers asked one of the ascetics: 'Why not come to us?' so he replied: 'I fear that should you bring me close, you would tempt me, and should you keep me away, you would deprive me. But your hand possesses nothing that I want and there is nothing in my hand that I fear losing. Those who have come to you have only come so that they would not need others because of you, and I do not need you because of Him who has made in no need of me.'

It is clear from these reports that accompanying the rulers is abhorrent. Furthermore, those who visit the rulers are subject to disobeying Allāh Mighty and Sublime either through his actions, speech, or silence.

[11] Abū Dāwūd #2860 on the authority of Abū Hurayrah (*raḍiy-Allah 'anhu*). There is an unknown narrator in the isnād. The first part has a corroborative report from Ibn 'Abbās (*raḍiy-Allāh 'anhumā*) and is ṣaḥīḥ.

As for actions, it is due to the fact that visiting the ruler usually entails stepping on stolen property. Should we assume that the property would not be stolen, what will be under him or the tent or whatever else that shades him is usually earned by his unlawful money and using that is impermissible. If we would assume those things would not be unlawful either, he is still at risk of committing other sins like prostrating to him, standing in his presence, serving him, or humbling himself to him because of the ruler-ship that he uses to oppress the people.

Humbling oneself for an oppressor is a sin. In fact, if one humbles himself for a wealthy person because of his wealth and for no other reason that necessitates humility, a third of his religion is wasted. With this in mind, how grave would it be to humble oneself to an oppressor?!

Kissing his hand is sinful as well unless one fears him. This is not the case with a just Caliph or a scholar who deserves that. As for others, one is only permitted to greet them.

As for speech, it is due to the fact that he might supplicate for the oppressor, praise him, or approve of his false words either directly, by nodding his head, or by a cheerful face. He might also express love and loyalty to him, manifest a yearning to meet him, and wish a long life for him. This is because in most cases the guest does not merely greet the ruler but speaks as well. His words will not go pass the aforementioned categories.

A report states: 'If someone supplicates for the long life of an oppressor, he wants Allāh to be disobeyed.'[12]

He is not allowed to supplicate for him except by saying something

[12] Al-'Irāqī says in *Takhrij al-Iḥyā'*, vol.2, pp.87: "I did not find it raised to the Prophet (ﷺ); it is only narrated by Ibn Abī al-Dunyā in *al-Ṣamt* as a statement of Al-Ḥasan.

like: "May Allāh rectify you" or "may Allāh direct you towards what is good."

As for silence, it is due to the fact that he might go to the gathering and see things like furniture of silk, vessels of silver, and boys with forbidden clothes of silk and remain silent. Anyone who sees these things and does not say anything is actually taking part in the sin. Similarly, he might hear them say vile things and lie, slander, and harm others with their tongues. Staying silent about that is impermissible because commanding what is right and rebuking what is wrong is obligatory upon him.

If you now say that his silence is excusable because he fears for himself, we say that you are right, but the fact remains that he has no need to subject himself to the unlawful without an excuse. If he does not visit him and witness these things, he is not obliged to command and rebuke anything. If one knows the corruption of a place and knows his inability to change it by attending, he is not allowed to enter.

Section Fourth:

Going to tyrannical rulers Due to an Excuse

Were we to assume that he is spared from all that has been mentioned-and farfetched that is indeed-he will not be spared from the corruption that finds its way to him when he sees their indulgence in pleasure. The likely consequences are that he will find himself belittling the blessings (*ni'ma*) that Allāh has bestowed upon him. Furthermore, others will follow his example in visiting to the ruler so he will be increasing the followers of the oppressors.

It has been narrated that Sa'īd Ibn al-Musayyib was once invited to pledge his allegiance (*bay'ah*) to al-Walīd and Sulaymān, the two sons of 'Abdu'l-Mālik but he said: 'I shall not give my pledge to two [at the same time] for as long as night follows the day.'[13] Then they said: 'Enter from this door and exist from the other!' but he said: 'No, by Allāh, I will not let anyone follow my example in that!' As a result, he was flogged one hundred lashes and dressed in the rough woolen garment.

Based on what has been mentioned, there are only two excuses for going to tyrannical rulers:

1. They demand that and their harm is feared if one refuses.
2. One goes to them to stops a Muslim from being oppressed. If this is the case, entering their presence is allowed on the condition that one does not lie and praise and does not neglect advice if he thinks it might be accepted.

This is what pertains to the ruling of going to the rulers.

Second, that the ruler comes to visit you himself: in this case, one is obliged to answer his greeting. As for standing up and honoring him for the honorable treatment he has given, it is not unlawful here. This is because the way he has honored knowledge and the religion makes him deserving of praise just as the way he has oppressed people makes him deserving of rebuke. If the ruler enters alone and the host deems it good to stand up in honor of the religion, that is better than sitting. If he enters with a group of men, then considering the dignified status that the governors enjoy among their people is even better, so there is nothing wrong in standing up with this intention. If, however, he knows that sitting down will not cause trouble within the people and that he will not be harmed by an upset ruler, it is better not to honor him by standing up. After this, he is obliged

[13] This is a beneficial point. Refer to my paper titled *al-Bay'a bayn al-Sunnah wa'l-Bid'ah*. Amman: Al-Maktaba al-Islamī.

to advise the ruler and to inform him about his unlawful activities if he does not know the ruling.

As for telling him that oppression and drinking wine are wrong, there is no benefit in that. What he must do instead is warn him of sinfulness as much as he thinks will affect his heart. He must also give him direction towards the best interest of all. If he knows of a legal way for the oppressor to get what he wants he tells him about it.

Third, that you stay away from them so that neither of you see each other: this is the safest way. He must hate their oppression with certain conviction. He must not desire to meet them and must not feel bad about anything he might miss due to not being in their presence. One of the pious said: 'There is but one day between me and the kings. As for the day that has passed, they cannot find its pleasure, while both I and they are fearful about tomorrow. It is but today-and who knows what will happen today!'

Issue: If a ruler sends you money and tells you to distribute it to the poor, you are not allowed to take it if its owner is known. If the owner is not known, the ruling is that he should give it in charity as mentioned earlier. Thus, he should go on and distribute it to the poor. Some scholars, however, refused to take money like this. If most of their money is unlawful, dealing with them is impermissible.

When it comes to the bridges, masjids, and drinking places built by the oppressors, the matter should be looked into: if the things used to build them belong to a specific owner, they can only be walked on in cases of necessity, but if the owner is not known, they can be used normally. A prudent person, however, refrains from that in both cases.

And Allāh knows best.

Chapter Five

On the Ethics in Companionship and Brotherhood

Know that harmony and union is the fruit (*thamar*) of good character (*ḥusn al-khuluq*) while disunity stems from bad character (*sū' al-khuluq*). This is simply because good character leads to mutual love (*taḥābub*) and agreement (*tawāfuq*) while bad character only sow the seed of mutual hatred (*tabāghuḍ*) and turning away (*tadābur*) from each other. The virtues (*faḍl*) of good character are obvious and there are many traditions about this.

It is narrated from Abū'l-Dardā' (*raḍiy Allāh 'anhu*) that the Prophet (ﷺ)said: "Nothing weighs more in a believer's scale on the Day of Resurrection than good character (*khuluq ḥasan*)."[1]

Another ḥadīth says: "Those of you whom I love the most and who shall sit nearest to me on the Day of Resurrection are those with the best character. Those of you whom I hate the most and

[1] Tirmidhī #2003; and Abū Dāwūd #4799 with a ḥasan isnād.

who shall sit farthest away from me on the Day of Resurrection are those with the worst character."[2]

When the Prophet (ﷺ) was asked what allows people to enter Paradise the most, he said: "Fear of Allāh and good character."[3]

With regard to love (*maḥabba*) for Allāh's sake, it occurs in the Two Ṣaḥīḥs from Abū Hurayrah (*raḍiy-Allāh 'anhu*) that the Prophet (ﷺ) said: "There are seven whom Allāh will bring under His shade on the day when there is no shade but His." These include: "Two men who loved each other for Allāh's sake; they came together upon that and separated upon that."[4]

In another ḥadīth, Allāh says: "My love is necessary for those who love each other for My sake, My love is necessary for those who give gladly to each other for My sake, and my love is necessary for those who visit each other for My sake."[5]

Another ḥadīth says: "The firmest handle of faith (*īmān*) is that you love for Allāh and hate for Allāh."[6] There are many ḥadīths to this effect.

Know that whoever loves for Allāh also hates for Allāh. After all, if

[2] Aḥmad, vol.4, pp.193; and al-Mundhirī: *al-Targhīb*, vol.3, pp.412 saying: 'It was narrated by Aḥmad from the narrators of the *al-Ṣaḥīḥ* as well as Ṭabarānī and Ibn Ḥibbān in his *al-Ṣaḥīḥ*.' A ḥadīth on the topic has also been related from Jābir (*raḍiy-Allāh 'anhu*) and Abū Hurayrah (*raḍiy-Allāh 'anhu*).

[3] Tirmidhī #2004 on the authority of Abū Hurayrah (*raḍiy-Allāh 'anhu*). Its corroborative texts render it ḥasan.

[4] Bukhārī, vol.2, pp.119; Muslim #1031; Mālik, vol.2, pp.952; Tirmidhī #2392; and Nasā'ī, vol.8, pp.22.

[5] Mālik, vol.2, pp.953 with a ṣaḥīḥ isnād from Mu'adh Ibn Jabal (*raḍiy-Allāh 'anhu*).

[6] Ṭabarānī: *al-Kabir* #11537; it has weakness in it, but al-Ṭayālisī relates a corroborative text from Ibn Mas'ūd (*raḍiy-Allāh 'anhu*), #378, and *al-Saghir*, vol.1, pp.224; Aḥmad on the authority of al-Barā' (*raḍiy-Allāh 'anhu*), vol.4, pp.286; and Ibn Abī Shayba: *al-Imān* #110. It is ḥasan by the latter two. Refer to: *al-Silsilah al-Ṣaḥīḥah* #1728.

you love a person because he is obedient to Allāh, you will certainly hate him for Allāh's sake if he disobeys Him. This is because anyone who loves another for some reason also hates him when the opposite of that reason occurs. This said, when one has both praiseworthy (*maḥmūda*) and abhorrent (*makrūha*) qualities, you must love him from one angle and hate him from another.

You must love a Muslim for his Islām and hate him for his disobedience and observe a middle way with him between total avoidance (*inqibāḍ*) and total relaxation (*istirsāl*). If his sin is just a slip and you know that he will regret it, it is better to overlook (*ighmāḍ*) and conceal (*sitr*) it. But if he persists in it, one must manifest his hate (*bughḍ*) by turning away (*i'rāḍ*), keeping distance (*tabā'ud*), and employing harsh words (*taghlīẓ al-qawl*) according to the harshness of the sin (*ghilaẓ al-ma'aṣiya*).

Know that those who go against Allāh's command are of different types:

The first type is an unbeliever (*kāfir*): if he is a warmonger (*ḥarbī*), he deserves to be disciplined or put into captivity. There is no humiliation beyond these two. If he is a subject of the Muslim state, the only harm that can be done to him is avoidance and scorn by forcing him to the narrow side of the road and not greeting him first. If he greets a Muslim by salām, the reply is: "*'alaykum* -and upon you."

It is best to refrain from accompanying him and dealing and eating with him. It is disliked to be totally relaxed and joyful with him like one is with friends.

The second type is an innovator (*mubtadi'*): if he invites others to accept an innovation (*bid'ah*) that leads to apostasy, his case is more severe than that of the non-Muslim subject because unlike a non-

Muslim subject, he cannot be made to pay the *jizya* and is not excused by a contract. If the innovation is not of the sort that renders one an apostate, his case is undoubtedly less serious than that of an unbeliever, but this is regarding the relation between him and Allāh. As for the rebuke that he faces, it is more severe than that faced by an unbeliever because the mischief of the latter affects him alone as no one cares what he says. This is not the case with an innovator who tells others to follow him as he claims that his views are correct and is thus a potential reason for the misguidance of others. Because the mischief of his innovation affects others, the hate, cutting of relations, enmity, scorn, condemnation, and warning is more severe.

The issue is lighter with a layman innovator who has no ability to invite others to adopt his views and nobody fears that he will gain followers. It is better to give gentle advice to a person like this, for the hearts of the laypeople are quick to change. If advising him does not help and one holds that avoiding him will make him realize the ugly nature of his innovation, there is no doubt that turning away from him is recommended. If one knows that this would have no effect because of the person's stubbornness and firm conviction, it is still best to turn away. This is simple due to the fact that if the vileness of innovation is not magnified, it will spread among the people and ruin them.

The third type is a sinner (*'āṣī*) who does not believe his sin is permissible: if the sin is of the type that affects others like oppression (*ẓulm*), forceful seizure (*ghaṣb*), false witness (*shahādat al-zūr*), backbiting (*ghība*), and slander (*namīma*), it is best to turn away from him by abstaining from his company and any dealings with him. The same applies to a person who incites others to adopt corruptive ways by, for example, bringing men and women together and facilitating drinking for the corrupt. Such people should be humiliated and all ties to them should be cut.

The matter is not as severe with someone who sins by himself by drinking wine (*khamr*), fornicating (*zinā*), stealing, or neglecting an obligation (*wājib*), but if he is caught in the act, he must be stopped with what is necessary. If advice makes him stop and helps him the most, he should be advised, but if it is of no use, harshness is resorted to.

Section One:
Exposition on What Must Be Considered When Choosing Companionship

It has been narrated that the Prophet (ﷺ) said: "A man is upon the ways of his friend (*khalīl*), so let each one of you look whom he takes as a friend."[7]

Know that not everyone qualifies for companionship (*ṣuḥba*); the person one chooses to spend time with should possess the traits (*ṣifāt*) that attract his company. These traits (*khiṣāl*) depend on the benefits (*fawā'id*) that one wishes to gain from the companionship. They can be worldly (*dunyawiyya*) like one's wealth (*māl*), status (*jāh*), or mere affection (*isti'nās*) through seeing (*mushāhada*) and discussing (*muḥāwara*), which is not what we wish to discuss here, or they can be religious (*dīniyya*). There are many ways one can benefit when it comes to his companion's religion. He can benefit from his knowledge (*'ilm*) and action (*'aml*) and his status can protect him from the harm of those who ruins people's hearts and distract them from worship (*'ibāda*). He can benefit from his wealth if it spares him from wasting time in seeking provisions. He can also seek his help (*isti'anah*) in carrying out important tasks, which makes him an asset in times of hardship

[7] Abū Dāwūd #4833; and Tirmidhī #2379 with a ḥasan isnād.

(*masā'il*) and strength (*quwa*) in various situations. He can also benefit from him by hoping for his intercession (*shafā'ah*) in the Afterlife, for one of the predecessors said: 'Have many brothers, for each believer is allowed to intercede.'

For each of these benefits specific conditions must be fulfilled. In general, your preferred companion should have five qualities:

He should be a person of intelligence (*'aql*) and fine character. He must not be a shameless sinner (*fāsiq*), innovator, or a person who is greedy (*ḥariṣ*) for this world.

Intellect is one's capital. There is no good in the company of an idiot as he wants to help you but only ends up causing harm. What we mean by an intelligent person is someone who understands the reality of things either by himself or after someone explains to them.

With respect to fine character, it is a must, for many people are intelligent but are easily overtaken by anger (*ghadab*) and desire (*shahwa*). There is no good in the companionship of such a person.

As for a vile sinner, he does not fear Allāh, and if a person does no fear Allāh, one is not safe from his mischief and cannot trust him.

As for an innovator, it is feared that his companionship leads to accepting his innovation.

'Umar Ibn al-Khaṭṭāb (*raḍiy-Allāh 'anhu*) said: 'Accompany the brothers of truthfulness (*ṣidq*) and live under their wing, for they are an adornment in times of ease (*rakhā'*) and an asset in times of calamity (*balā'*). Think the best about your brother unless he comes to you with something that angers you. Stay away from your enemy.

Be cautious with your friend except for those who are trusted (*amīn*), and no one is trusted save those who fear Allāh. Do not accompany a sinner (*fājir*) and learn from his sinfulness as a result, and do not tell him your secrets. Consult those who fear Allāh regarding your affairs.'

Yaḥyā Ibn Mu'adh said: 'What a terrible friend someone is if you need to tell him: 'Remember me in your supplications!' or whom you need to live in fearful flattery with, or whom you need to present excuses to.'

Once a group of people went to al-Ḥasan and found him sleeping, and one of them began eating from the fruits that were in the house. When he saw this, he said: 'May Allāh have mercy on you! This, by Allāh, is what brothers do!'

Abū Ja'far once told his companions: 'Do some of you put his hand in his brother's pocket and take what he wishes?' They said: 'No.' So he said: 'Then you are not brothers as you claim.'

It has been narrated that Fath al-Mawsili once went to see a friend of his called 'Isā al-Tammār but he was not home. He then told the servant girl: 'Bring me my brother's purse.' She brought it and he took two dirhams from it. When 'Isa returned home, she told him what had happened. 'Isa said: 'If you are speaking the truth, you are free!' Then he looked (into the purse) and found that she was right. Then he freed her.

Section Two:

Exposition on the Rights of Brotherhood and Companionship

The first duty is to fulfill the needs (*ḥājāt*) of his brothers. This has different levels (*darajāt*), the lowest of which is helping them when they ask for help and one is able (*qudra*) to help. This should happen with cheerfulness (*bashāsha*) and good will (*istibshār*). The middle level is helping (*ḥawā'ij*) them before they even ask. The highest level is putting their needs before one's own needs. Indeed, one of our righteous predecessors used to take care of his friend's family for forty years after his death.

The second duty concerns supporting them with the tongue (*lisān*). This happens sometimes through silence (*sukūt*) and sometimes through speaking (*nutq*). With respect to silence, one should not speak about their faults (*'ayūb*) in their presence (*ḥadūr*) and absence (*ghaiba*) and should refrain from criticizing (*mumārāt*) them and disputing (*munāqasha*) with them. One should not ask his friends about affairs that they do not want to reveal and when he sees them, he must not say: "Where are you going?" for it might be that they do not wish to tell. One must keep their secrets even if the ties have been broken and must never revile one's loved ones and family. If someone speaks ill about them, he must not convey that to him.

The third duty: One should stay silent about anything they dislike unless talking is obligatory in order to command what is right and rebuke what is wrong and there is no excuse to stay silent. Confronting one's friend in a case like this is actually kindness (*iḥsān*) towards him.

Know that should you seek a companion who is free of faults (*'ayb*), you will never find one. The goal is to find someone whose good qualities are more than his bad ones.

Ibn al-Mubārak says: 'A believer (*mu'min*) looks for excuses while a hypocrite (*munāfiq*) looks for mistakes.'

Al-Fuḍayl said: 'Generosity means overlooking the slips of one's brothers.'

You should not think (*ẓann*) bad about your friend but should always make good excuses for his actions as much as possible. Indeed, the Prophet (ﷺ) said: "Beware of assumptions, for out of all speech assumptions are the falsest."[8]

Know that evil assumptions lead to unlawful spying (*tajjasus*)[9] and concealing the faults of other people and overlooking them is the natural quality (*shayma*)[10] of the religious.

Know that one's faith (*imān*) is not complete till he loves for his brother what he loves for himself. The lowest level of brotherhood (*ukhūwa*) entails treating your brother the way you would like others to treat you. This said, there is no doubt that you expect your brother to conceal your faults and remain silent about your bad sides, and should he act contradictory to that, you would be very upset. How then do you expect him to do for you what you are not determined to do for him?!

If you seek fairness from others but do not observe it yourself you are included in the verse:

---

[8] Bukhārī, vol.10, pp.403; Muslim #2559; Mālik, vol.2, pp.907; Abū Dāwūd #4910; and Tirmidhi #1936 on the authority of Abū Hurayrah (*raḍiy Allah 'anhu*).

[9] As occurs in the last part of the aforementioned hadīth: "And do not spy."

[10] The Shāmiyyah edition reads: "Sima (sign)." The correct wording is taken from *al-Iḥya'*, vol.2, pp.178.

ٱلَّذِينَ إِذَا ٱكْتَالُوا۟ عَلَى ٱلنَّاسِ يَسْتَوْفُونَ ۝٢ وَإِذَا كَالُوهُمْ أَو وَّزَنُوهُمْ يُخْسِرُونَ ۝٣

"Who, when they take a measure from people, take in full. But if they give by measure or by weight to them, they cause loss."
[*al-Mutaffifin* (83): 2-3]

The reason behind neglecting one's duty to conceal other people's faults and being tempted to expose them is rancor (*ḥiqd*) and jealousy (*ḥasad*).

Know that one of the major reasons behind rancor and jealousy between brothers (*ikhwān*) is disputation which only occurs when people attempt to stand out as more virtuous and more intelligent than others and scorn those they criticize. Whoever disputes with his brother is actually calling him ignorant (*jahl*) and stupid (*ḥamq*) or someone who is heedless (*ghafla)* and oblivious (*sahw*) of the reality of something. All of that is a form of belittlement (*istiḥqār*) and as such creates ill feelings and enmity between people, which is the opposite of brotherhood.

The fourth duty is to use the tongue for speaking out. As brotherhood necessitates not mentioning that which your companion dislikes, it also requires to say that which is beneficial and good. This is more emphasized in the case of friends because if a person is contend with having a friend who refrains from saying what he dislikes, then he should accompany the dwellers of graves (i.e. they will not hurt him with any word since they cannot speak). The reason people choose to have friends and companions is that benefit is sought from such relationship because controlling the tongue means to protect your companions from the harm of your tongue. Thus, one should employ his tongue to make amorous advances towards his companion and check on him and show his concerns if he is concerned and happiness if he is happy.

It was narrated in the authentic ḥadīth that the Prophet (ﷺ) said: "If a person loves his brother then he should inform him of that."[11]

This includes calling him with names that he loves the most. 'Umar Ibn al-Khaṭṭāb (*raḍiy-Allāh 'anhu*) said: 'Three things make your brother's love (*wadd*) for you pure: that you greet him when you see him, that you give him space in a gathering, and that you call him with his names that you love the most.'

This also includes praising him for his fine qualities that one is aware of when that influences those who are present. One should also praise his children, family, and actions. In fact, the principle applies even to his character, intellect, appearance, handwriting, authoring, and everything that causes joy as long as one does not go too far and does not speak lies.

You should also tell him if someone else has praised him and show him your happiness for that. Hiding something like this is pure jealousy.

This also includes thanking him for what he has done for you and defending him in his absence if somebody speaks ill about him. The duties of brotherhood include readiness to protect and help each other.

It occurs in a sound ḥadīth: "A Muslim is the brother of another Muslim; he does not wrong him and he does not forsake him."[12]

---

[11] Tirmidhī #2393 and Abū Dāwūd #5124; It is authentic as stated by the author.

[12] Bukhārī, vol.5, pp.70; Muslim #2580; and Tirmidhī #1426 on the authority of Ibn 'Umar (*raḍiy-Allāh 'anhu*).

Whenever a person neglects defending the honor of his brother, he has forsaken him. To estimate the situation, consider it from two angles:

Firstly, assume that what is being said about him would be said about you in his presence-then say what you would like him to say.

Secondly, assume that he is listening behind the wall-whatever your heart (*qalb*) would tell you to say in his defense in his presence, it should tell you the same in his absence. If one is not sincere (*mukliṣ*) in his brotherhood, he is a hypocrite.

The example of this is forgiving (*afuu*) his errs, if his err was in a matter related to religion, then do not give up on him and continue advising him and admonishing him, but kindly; if he insists on his mistakes then show him sternness (*musārama*).

The fifth duty is to supplicate (*du'ā'*) for your brother, during his life and after his death, and you should supplicate for him as you supplicate for yourself.

Abū'l-Dardā' (*raḍiy.Allāh 'anhu*) narrated that the Prophet (ﷺ) said: "The supplication of a Muslim for his brother in his absence is readily accepted, an angel is appointed to his side, whenever he makes a beneficial supplication for his brother the appointed angel says: '*Āmīn*' and may you also be blessed with the same"[13]

Abū'l-Dardā' (*raḍiy.Allāh 'anhu*) used to supplicate for many of his companions, mentioning each one by his name in the supplication.

Aḥmad ibn Ḥanbal (may Allāh have mercy on him) used to sup-

[13] Muslim #2732 and Abū Dāwūd #1534.

plicate for six people in the later portion of the night.

As for supplicating for one's companions after their death, 'Amr ibn Huraith said: 'If a person supplicates for his deceased friend, an angel will carry his supplication to his grave and say: 'O stranger living in the grave! This is a gift from a concerned friend (*shaqiq*) of yours.'[14]

The sixth duty is to be loyal (*wafā'*) and sincere (*ikhlāṣ*). The meaning of loyalty is to keep the bond of love with the friend until he passes away, and after his death, to keep this bond with the children and friends of his deceased friend. The Prophet (ﷺ) honored an old woman and said: "She used to visit us at the time of Khadījah, and loyalty (*'ahd*) is part of faith (*īmān*)."[15]

From loyalty is to show humility (*tawāḍi'*) to brothers even after assuming better positions, higher status or more wealth.

Know that it is not from loyalty to accord with your brother in matters contravening religion. Al-Shāfi'ī (may Allāh have mercy on him) had a close companion called Muḥammad ibn 'Abd al-Ḥakam who he used to draw him near and embrace him. When al- Shāfi'ī was on his deathbed, he was asked about the one who he will appoint to take his place to teach people. On that moment, Muḥammad ibn 'Abd al-Ḥakam was sitting next to his head and started to show himself so that al- Shāfi'ī selects him. However, al-Shāfi'ī appointed Abū Ya'qūb al-Buwayṭī, which made Muḥammad, feels disappointed.

---

[14] This is not established neither in the Qur'ān nor Sunnah. Thus, this statement should not be considered.

[15] Al-Irāqī said in *'Takhrij al-Iḥyā"*, vol.2, pp.187: Ḥākim reported it from the hadīth of 'Ā'ishah (*radiy Allāh 'anha*) and then said: It is authentic according to the conditions of Bukhārī and Muslim, and it is free of defects. I say: Al-Ḥāfiẓ Ibn Ḥajr said in *Fatḥ al-Bārī*, vol.10, pp.436: "It was reported by Ḥākim and al-Bayhaqī from the way of Ṣāliḥ ibn Rustum... al-Bayhaqi reported it from the way of Salm ibn Janadah... and said it is gharīb, and from the way of Abū Salamah.... and its isnād is weak.

The reason he was not selected is that al-Buwayṭī was more pious and ascetic though Muḥammad was well versed in knowledge. The sincerity of al-Shāfiʿī and his loyalty to the Muslims made him select the best person for this job and did not let his friendship have any effect on his decision. This made Ibn ʿAbd al-Ḥakam change his *Madhhab* and follow the *Madhhab* of Imām Mālik.[16]

From loyalty is not to lend one's ear to the accusations of people against his friend (*ṣiddīq*) and not to befriend the enemy (*ʿadw*) of his friend.

The seventh duty is to not overburden his brother at all and make it easy on him, meaning one should not take advantage of his brother's status and wealth. Rather, one should take his mind from the stress of his duties and responsibilities. One should not make his brother feel obliged to check on him, fulfill his rights and show humbleness to him. Rather, the only motive for his love and relationship with him is the pleasure of Allāh alone and the hope to enjoy the blessings of his supplications (i.e. when supplicating for him) and enjoy his company and benefit from his religiousness and draw oneself near to Allāh through fulfilling his right, and remove all the barriers so that one deals with his brothers as if they are himself.

Jaʿfar ibn Muḥammad said: "The heaviest ones on my heart from my companions are those who overburden themselves for me and I do not feel comfortable to do or say anything I want in their presence. The lightest on my heart are those who I feel so free as I am alone when I am in their company.

A wise man said: A person who you do not feel to be formal with is a person who's your relationship with lasts. From the perfect characteristics in this issue is to see that your brothers have favors

[16] Al-Qāḍī Iyyāḍ refuted the claim in *Tartīb al-Madārik*, vol.3, pp.65.

on you and not the other way around, and so you deal with them as if you are their servants.

Section Three:

Exposition on the Etiquettes of Interaction with People

In this section I will mention a number of etiquettes (*ādāb*) related to how a person should deal and interact with people:

Part of the good social manners is to have an upright character without being proud (*kibr*), present a humble trait without being disgraced, and meet both friends and foes with a face of countenance without being humiliated or afraid of them. A person ought to avoid interlocking your fingers, putting your finger in your noise, spitting a lot, and yawning while you are in a gathering.

Listen to the person who is addressing you and refrain from asking the speaker to repeat what he said, and beware of sharing with others your admiration for your child, and your slave-girl. Do not adopt the mannerisms of a woman in prettying up yourself, and do not degrade yourself like a slave.

Make your family fear you without resorting to violence, and be lenient with them without being weak.

Do not joke with your female and male slave so you do not lose respect, and avoid constantly turn to look back.

Do not sit with the ruler, and if you do so be wary of sins and backbiting others. You should keep the ruler's secret and beware of joking, belching, and flossing your teeth in his presence. If he draws you near him be wary of him, and if he entrusted you and is open with, then do not feel assured that he will not turn against you. Be gentle with him as you are gentle to a small boy, speak that which pleases him, and do not interfere in issues between him and his family, and his entourage.

Beware of fair-weather friends.

Do not let your wealth be more valuable than your honor.

When you attend a gathering, make sure to sit where it is most likely to show humbleness.

Do not sit on the road side. If you do so, lower your gaze, help the oppressed, and guide the lost.

Do not spit in the direction of the qiblah nor to your right, rather spit to your left or under your left leg.

Be cautious of being in the company of the laymen, and if you do so, you should overlook their bad manners, and avoid participating in their conversation.

Beware of excessive joking, because an intelligent person will dislike you for it, and it will embolden a foolish person to disrespect you.

Section Four:

The Rights of Muslims, Kinship, Neighbours and Kings

Among the rights (*haqūq*) of a Muslim are to greet him when you meet him, respond to his invitation, when he sneezes and says,

الحَمْدُ لِلّٰهِ

"*alḥamdulillāh* (All praise is due to Allāh),"

you should say,

يَرْحَمُكَ اللّٰهُ

"*Yarḥamuk-Allāh* (may Allāh have mercy on you)".

You should attend his funeral, fulfill his oath, advise him when he seeks your advice, safeguard his honor when he is absent, like for him what you like for yourself, and dislike for him what you dislike for yourself. All these rights are stated in a number of ḥadīths.[17]

Other rights are to refrain from harming the Muslims with your words or actions, and be humble yourself to them and avoid being arrogant, and do not listen to the gossips of people against each other and do not share with others the information you hear from others.

As for other rights, they include: You should not desert or boycott (*hajr*) a Muslim you know for more than three days, because of a well-known ḥadīth on the issue.[18]

It is also narrated from Abū Hurayrah (*raḍiy-Allāh 'anhu*) that the Prophet (ﷺ) said: "It is not permissible for a believer to forsake his

[17] The ḥadīths are well- known and all of them are authentic and established..

[18] Bukhārī, vol.10, pp.403, Muslim #2559, Mālik, vol.2, pp.907, Abū Dāwūd #4910, and Tirmidhī #1936.

(Muslim) brother for more than three days. If three days have passed, he should meet him and greet him; and if the other responds to it they will both share the reward; but if he does not respond, he will bear his sin and the one who (has taken the initiative to) greet (the other) will be absolved of the sin of forsaking (one's brother in faith)."[19]

Know that this forsaking of a person (mentioned above) is concerning worldly issues. As for the rights of religion; the forsaking of the people of innovation (*ahlul-bid'ah*), and the people of vain desires (*ahlul-hawā'*) and the people disobedient (*ahlul-mā'ṣī*); it should be permanent, if they do not repent (*tawba*) or return (*rajū'*) to the right path.[20]

Part of the rights of a Muslim are: that a Muslim should help and do any good that he is able to do for other Muslims, and he should not go into any Muslim's house except after getting permission from the owner of the house to enter. A person should seek permission to enter a house three times, if the permission is not granted the person should leave.

Other rights of the Muslims are: that a Muslim should behave decently towards people, and that is by dealing with each person in a manner that befits them. This is because a person, who talks with an ignorant person about scholarship; an idle person about rulings; and a foolish person with elucidation, will harm you and harm others.

More rights of a Muslim are: that he should respect the elderly and show mercy to the youngsters. He should display a smiling counte-

[19] Abū Dāwūd #4912, and it is a weak ḥadīth. However, supporting evidence strengthen this ḥadīth. It was graded as authentic by al-Ḥāfiẓ ibn Ḥajr al-'Asqalānī in *al-Fath*, vol.10, pp.413.
[20] Imām al-Suyūṭi wrote an epistle solely for this issue. It is entitled *al-Zajr bi'l-Hajr*. A manuscript of this book is in the 'Ārif Ḥikmat bookshop in Medīnah.

nance to everyone and he should be gentle with all people. He should fulfill his promises, be just to people and treat them as he himself would like to be treated.

Al-Ḥasan said, 'Allāh revealed four things to Ādam (*'alayhis-salām*), and He said, "These things are the basis of all things for you and your children. One of which is for Me, another one is for you, one is between Me and you, and the other is between you and the people". As for the thing that is for Me; it is that you must worship Me (alone) and not associate anything in worship with Me. The thing that is for you is that I will reward you for your deeds when you are most in need of the reward. The thing that is between Me and you is that you should supplicate to Me and I will answer your supplications. As for the thing that is between you and the people; it is that you should treat them as you would like them to treat you."'

More rights are that: there should be additional respect for people of status, and settle the disputes between people and bring them into harmony, and hide the faults of the Muslims.

Know that a person who ponders on Allāh's covering up of the misdeeds of the sinners in the world should embrace His Compassion for He has dictated that the testimony for adultery should be given by four just witnesses who testify that they witnessed the sexual act and saw the man's private part in the woman's private part like a stick in a kohl jar, which is a condition that is unlikely to be possible. If this is the effect of His magnanimity in this worldly life, then the same ought to be anticipated from Him in the Afterlife.

Other rights include that a person should avoid putting himself in suspicious situations to protect the hearts of the people from the sin of thinking ill (*sū' al-ẓann*) about him, and safeguard their tongues from backbiting (*ghibah*) him.

The Muslim should intercede to a person of status on behalf of a Muslim who needs intercession, and he should strive to fulfil the needs of his fellow Muslims.

Other rights are that he should start by greeting before talking to other Muslims, and it is the Sunnah to shake his hand. It was narrated that Anas (*raḍiy Allāh ʿanhu*) transmitted that the Prophet (ﷺ) said, "If any two Muslims meet, and they both shake hands, Allāh will make it incumbent upon Himself to listen attentively to their supplication, and by the time that they separate their hands Allāh will have forgiven them."[21]

Another ḥadīth states: "When a believer greets another believer, one hundred mercies will descend upon them, ninety-nine of them will be for the one who smiled more and is the better of the two in character."[22]

It is permissible to kiss the hand of a person who is revered in Islām, and there is nothing wrong with embracing each other. As for getting hold of the reins of a riding camel; this was done by Ibn ʿAbbās (*raḍiy Allāh ʿanhumā*) for Zayd Ibn Thābit (*raḍiy Allāh ʿanhu*). To stand to show respect to and honour the honourable people is good.[23] However, bowing is prohibited.

[21] Aḥmad, vol.2, pp.142. Al-Mundhirī mentioned this ḥadīth in *al-Targhīb*, vol.3, pp.270, and he said: 'The ḥadīth was transmitted by Aḥmad, al-Bazzār and Abū Ya'lā. All the narrators in the ḥadīth of Aḥmad are ṣaḥīḥ except Maymūn al-Mara'i. This is one of the ḥadīth s which was rejected because of Maymūn's weakness". Refer to *Majma' al-Zawā'id*, vol.8, pp.36.
[22] Ṭabarānī in *al-Awsat*. However, there is al-Ḥusayn ibn Kathīr in the isnād of narrators of this ḥadīth, and he is unknown. The rest of the narrators of the ḥadīth are ṣaḥīḥ. This is what al-Haythamī said in *al-Majma'*, vol.8, pp.37. Al-'Irāqī also mentioned the same in *al-Mughni*, vol.2, pp.204.
[23] This is contrary to the statement of Ibn ʿAbbās (*raḍiy Allāh ʿanhumā*) that: 'There was no person more beloved to them than the Messenger of Allāh (ﷺ).' [He said:] 'And they would not stand when they saw him because they knew that he disliked that.' This ḥadīth was transmitted by Bukhārī in *al-Adab al-Mufrad* #946, Tirmidhī, vol.2, pp.125, and Aḥmad, vol.3, pp.132. They all transmitted the ḥadīth with a ṣaḥīḥ isnād of narrators.

Some of the rights are: that a Muslim should protect the honour, life and wealth of Muslims from the oppression of others, and he should defend him and support him.

If a person is trialled by knowing an evil person, he should be courteous to him and avoid him based on the ḥadīth of 'Ā'ishah bint Abū Bakr (*raḍiy-Allāh 'anhumā*).[24]

Muḥammad Ibn al-Ḥanafiyyah said, 'A person who does not relate well to a person whom he cannot avoid until Allāh gives a way out for him is not wise.'

A person should avoid mixing with the rich, and he should mix with the poor, and be kind to the orphans.

He should visit the sick.

Amongst the etiquettes of visiting the sick is that a person should put his hand on the sick person, and ask him about his condition. It is part of the etiquettes to refrain from overstaying, be gentle, supplicate for the sick person's wellbeing, and lower his gaze and not stare at the blemishes at the place where the sick person is located.

It is recommended for the sick person to do what was transmitted by Muslim[25] in the ḥadīth of 'Uthmān ibn Abū'l- 'Āṣ (*raḍiy-Allāh 'anhu*) who complained to the Prophet (ﷺ) about pain that he was feeling in his body, and he had been feeling it since he embraced Islām. The Prophet (ﷺ), "Place your hand where you feel pain and say:

بِسْمِ اللهِ

[24] Bukhārī, vol.10, pp.438, and Muslim #2291, and the it states, 'One of the worst people in Allāh's sight on the day of Judgment will be a person whom people avoided because of his evilness.'
[25] Muslim #2202, and Mālik, vol.2, pp.942, Abū Dāwūd #3891 and Tirmidhī #2081.

'With the Name of Allāh'

three times; and then repeat seven times:

أَعُوذُ بِاللَّهِ وَقُدْرَتِهِ مِنْ شَرِّ مَا أَجِدُ وَأُحَاذِرُ

"I seek refuge with Allāh and with His Power from the evil that afflicts me and that which I apprehend."

The etiquettes that the sick should observe are: He should have good patience *(ḥasan al-ṣabr)*, refrain from complaining *(qila al-shakwa)* or displaying displeasure *(faza')*, resort to supplication *(du'ā')* and depend *(tawakkul)* on Allāh.

The Muslim should walk in the funeral of the deceased and visit their graves. The objective of walking in the funerals of Muslims is to fulfill their rights and contemplate death.

Al-A'mash said, 'We used to attend funerals and we could not recognize the family of the deceased to console them because everyone seemed to be immersed in grief.'

The objective of visiting the graves is to supplicate,[26] contemplate and soften the heart *(tarqīq al-qalb)*.

Some of the etiquettes related to following the [funeral of] the decease are: walking behind it, maintaining humility *(khushū')* before Allāh, refrain from talking, observing the deceased, thinking *(tafqīr)* about death and preparing for it.

The rights of the neighbour *(ḥaqūq al-jār)*: It is worth to acknowledge that the neighbour is entitled to a right that is more than the

[26] There is no basis for reciting the Qur'ān at the graveyard as is done by some people.

right of the brotherhood in Islām. Thus, the neighbour deserves more than the right is due to every Muslim in normal situations. It is narrated that the Prophet (ﷺ) said "There are three types of neighbours; a neighbour who has one right, a neighbour who has two rights, and a neighbour who has three rights. The neighbour who has three rights is a Muslim neighbour who is also a relative. He has the right of neighbourliness, the right of Islām and the right of kinship. The neighbour who has two rights is the Muslim neighbour. He has the right of Islām, and the right of neighbourliness. The neighbour who has one right is the neighbour who is a polytheist."

Know that the right of neighbourliness is not only to refrain from harming him, rather, it extends to include forbearing his harm, being gentle to him, initiating the good, greeting him first, avoiding talking for too long with him, visiting him when he is sick, consoling him at times of affliction, congratulating him at times of happiness, overlooking his faults, not looking into his house, not disturbing him by hitting a wooden peg into a shared wall, not pouring water into his drain, and not throwing dust into his courtyard. A Muslim should not look at what his neighbour carries to his house, he should cover up his neighbour's shortcomings, he should not eavesdrop on his conversations, he should lower his gaze when he sees his neighbour's women, and he should cater for the needs of his neighbour's family when he is away.

Section Five:
The rights of the relatives and kinsmen

Concerning the rights of the relatives (*al-aqārib*) and kinsmen (*al-raḥm*), an authentic narration from 'Ā'ishah (*raḍiy.Allāh 'anhā*) states, that the Prophet (ﷺ) said: "The bond of relationship is suspending from the Throne (*'arsh*), and says: 'He who keeps good relations with me, Allāh will keep connection with him, but whosoever severs relations with me, Allāh will sever connection with him.'"[27]

Another ḥadīth by Bukhārī[28] states: "The person who perfectly maintains the ties of kinship is not the one who does it because he gets recompensed by his relatives (for being kind and good to them), but the one who truly maintains the bonds of kinship is the one who persists in doing so even though the latter has severed the ties of kinship with him."

Another ḥadīth transmitted by Muslim states that a man said, "I have relatives with whom I try to keep the ties of relationship with but they sever relations with me; and whom I treat kindly but they treat me badly, I am gentle with them but they are rough to me." He (ﷺ) replied, "If you are as you say, it is as if you are feeding them hot ashes, and you will be with a supporter against them from Allāh as long as you continue to do so."

This means: you will be supported against them. They will not be able to argue that the person did not fulfill the right of kinship, and the person upon who hot ashes are thrown will be not be able to talk. There are many well-known aḥādīth concerning maintaining ties of

[27] Bukhārī, vol.10, pp.350, and Muslim #2555.
[28] Bukhārī, vol.10, pp.355, Abū Dāwūd #1297, and Tirmidhī #1909.

kinship (*silat al-raḥm*), the rights of the parents (*ḥaqūq al-walidayn*),[29] and emphasizing the right of the mother.

As for the rights of the child (*ḥaqūq al-walad*): It is noteworthy that due to the fact that a person is naturally inclined to his child, there was no need to emphasize the advice of treating him well. However, the parent's love for the child may be excessive and he will neglect teaching his child and disciplining him. Allāh said:

$$قُوٓا۟ أَنفُسَكُمْ وَأَهْلِيكُمْ نَارًا$$

"Protect yourselves and your families from Fire"

[*al-Taḥrīm*: 6]

The scholars of *tafsīr*[30] said, 'This means: teach them and discipline them.'

The parent must choose a good name for his child; slaughter an animal to celebrate his birth (the rite of *'aqīqah*[31]). When the child reaches the age of seven, the parent should command him to perform prayer (*salāh*) and circumcise him. When the child becomes an adult, the parent should marry him off.

The rights for the governed (*ḥaqūq al-mamlūk*) are that they should be fed, and clothed, not commanded to do things which are beyond their capacity, nor look down upon, and forgive their mistakes. He should remember Allāh when they errs, and forgives, hoping that Allāh will also forgive him.

---

[29] Shaykh Naẓām Sakjaha has two beneficial epistles on this topic. One of them is a manuscript, and the other is a published book.
[30] *Zād al-Masīr*, vol.8, pp.312.
[31] An *'aqīqah* is slaughtering an animal for the new-born baby on his seventh day. Two sheep are slaughtered for a boy, and one sheep is slaughtered for a girl. *Tuḥfat al-Mawlūd* by Ibn al-Qayyim, *Thalāth Sha'ā'ir* by 'Umar Sulaymān al-'Ashqar.

Chapter Six

On the Ethics of Solitude

The scholars have differed on whether solitude (*'uzla*) or mixing with people (*mukhālata*) is better? This is despite the fact that each of these things has benefits (*fawā'id*) and pitfalls (*ghawā'il*). Most of the ascetics (*zuhhād*) were of the opinion that solitude is better.

Those who chose solitude include Sufyān al-Thawrī, Ibrāhīm Ibn 'Adham, Dāwūd al-Ṭā'i, al-Fuḍayl [Ibn 'Iyyāḍ], Bishr al-Ḥāfī and others.

Those who said that mixing with people is recommended include Sa'īd ibn al-Musayyab, Shurayḥ, al-Sha'bī, ['Abdullāh] Ibn al-Mubārak and others.

Both groups of scholars have evidence to support their stance and I will indicate some of it.

The evidence by the first group of scholars is what was transmitted in the Two Ṣaḥīḥs[1] from the ḥadīths of Abū Sa'īd (*raḍiy-Allāh 'anhu*) where he said: 'Who is the best among men?' The Prophet (ﷺ) replied, "A believer who strives in the way of Allāh with his wealth and life." The man asked again: 'Who is next to him (in excellence)?' The Prophet (ﷺ) said: "Next to him is a man who is engaged in worshipping his Lord in a mountain valley, leaving the people secure from his mischief."

A ḥadīth by 'Uqbah ibn 'Āmir (*raḍiy-Allāh 'anhu*) in which 'Uqbah said: 'I said: 'O Messenger of Allāh! What is the means to salvation?' He (ﷺ) said: "That you control your tongue let your house suffice for you, and cry over your sins."[2]

'Umar Ibn al-Khaṭṭāb (*raḍiy-Allāh 'anhu*) said: 'Set aside some time where you isolate yourself.'

Sa'd Ibn Abi Waqqāṣ (*raḍiy-Allāh 'anhu*) said, 'Indeed, I wish that there was a steel door between me and people so that no one would speak to me and I would not speak to anyone until I (died, became resurrected) and met Allāh.

Ibn Mas'ūd (*raḍiy-Allāh 'anhu*) said: 'Be fountains of knowledge, sources of guidance, confined to your houses, vigorous in the worship of Allāh, have old clothes, be known to the inhabitants of heaven, and be unknown to the inhabitants of the earth.'

Abū'l-Dardā' (*raḍiy-Allāh 'anhu*) said: 'A person's house is a good hermitage for him, it safeguards his tongue, his private parts and his eyesight. Beware of gatherings in the markets, because they distract and cause error."

[1] Bukhārī vol.6, pp.6, and Muslim #1888.

[2] Tirmidhī #2408, Aḥmad, vol.4, pp.148, vol.4, pp.259, Ṭabarānī in *al-Kabīr* #740, #741, and Ibn al-Mubārak in *al-Zuhd* #134. This ḥadīth is ṣaḥīḥ.

Dāwūd al-Ṭā'i said: 'Flee from people as you would flee from a lion.'

Abū'l-Muhalhal said: 'Sufyān al-Thawrī held my hand and took me out to the desert. He led me to a secluded place. Then he cried and said: 'O Abū'l-Muhalhal! If you can manage to avoid mixing with anyone at all in this time, then do so. Be concerned with rectifying (*maramma*) yourself.'

The proofs of those who were of the opinion that mixing with people is recommended include the statement of the Prophet (ﷺ): "A believer who mixes with people and endures their annoyance is better than the one who does not mix with them and does not endure their annoyance."[3]

They had other proofs which cannot be validly used to establish their position like Allāh's statement:

وَلَا تَكُونُوا كَالَّذِينَ تَفَرَّقُوا وَاخْتَلَفُوا

> "And do not be like the ones who became divided and differed."
>
> [*Āl-'Imrān* (3): 105]

However, using this *ayah* as evidence is not valid because what is meant by difference in the *ayah* is difference of views and opinions in the principles of religion.

These scholars also used as evidence the Prophet's (ﷺ) statement: "A Muslim should not forsake his (Muslim) brother for more than three days."[4]

---

[3] Tirmidhī, vol.3, pp.319, Bukhārī in *al-Adab al-Mufrad* #388, Aḥmad #5022 and Abū Nu'aym, vol.7, pp.365.

[4] Bukhārī, vol.10, pp.403, Muslim #2559, Mālik, vol.2, pp.907, Abū Dāwūd #4910 and Tirmidhī #1936.

They said that solitude is complete forsaking of Muslims. However, this is not a strong argument because what the ḥadīth means is that it is prohibited to desist from talking to Muslims, greeting them and ordinary mixing with them.[5]

Section One:

On the Benefits of Solitude, and its Pitfalls, and showing the truth about the superiority of solitude

Know that the difference of opinion of scholars in this issue is like their difference of opinion on the virtues of marriage and bachelorhood. I have previously mentioned that this issue differs according to the conditions of people. This is exactly as I say in this issue.

Firstly, I will mention the benefits of bachelorhood, and they are six:

The first benefit: It allows the person to be free to worship (*'ibādah*). Additionally, one can find pleasure in supplicating to Allāh because this requires the person to be free from distractions, while there is no free time for a person who mixes with people. It is for this reason; solitude is a means (*wasila*) whereby this purpose is achieved especially in the beginning.

A wise man was asked: 'Where did asceticism (*zuhd*) and solitude (*khalwa*) lead the worshippers to?' He said: 'Finding intimacy (*uns*) in [the worship of] Allāh.'

Uways al-Qarnī said: 'I do not believe that a person who finds tranquility and intimacy in the worship of his Lord will ever find the

[5] In *Riyād al-Sālihīn*, p.264, Imām al-Nawawī wrote the chapter heading which states: Chapter: The preference of isolation in corrupt times. I said: '*Insha'-Allāh*, this is the well-versed opinion on the issue.'

same in anything else.'

Know that if a person has facilitated for himself in finding pleasure in the worship of Allāh through constant remembrance (*dhikr*) of Allāh or acquiring the knowledge of Allāh through constant contemplation, then dedicating to that is better than all the things associated with mixing with people.

The second benefit: Solitude entails isolating one from sins (*'uzla 'an'l-ma'āṣī*) which often are committed as a result of mixing with people. These sins are four:

First, this concerns backbiting (*ghība*), because the custom of the people is to rinse their mouths with talking about the honor of other people and to engage in backbiting for fun. Thus, if you mix with people and engage with them in their talks, you are bound to sin, and be exposed to the wrath of Allāh. If you decided to remain quiet while other people are engaging in backbiting you will still be their partner in crime, because a person who listens to backbiting is considered to be one of the backbiters. If you admonished them for their backbiting they will hate you, backbite you in return and thus accumulate their number of backbiting, let alone the fact that they may also revile you.

Second, this is related to commanding people to do the good and preventing them from evil (*al-amr b'il-ma'rūf wa'l-nahyi 'an'l-munkar*), because if a person mixes with people he cannot but witness evil; hence if he does not speak against it he will be sinful, and if he stands against it he will be exposed to different types of harm. Indeed, solitude makes a person safe from all this.

Third, it is associated with ostentatious (*riyā'*); a serious illness that is difficult to avoid. The first problem in mixing with people is that a person has to show a desire for meeting the people, which always involves untruthfulness in some way or another i.e. either the person does not desire to meet them but has to pretend that he is sincere or he desires to meet them but exaggerates in showing that. The righteous predecessors were careful when responding to questions like, "How are you this morning?" and "How are you this evening?" When one of the predecessors was asked, "How is your morning?" he replied, "I woke up this morning while I am weak and sinful, consuming my provision and waiting for my appointed tie (to die)."

Know that if a person asks another, "How are you this morning?" while the inquiry is not made due to one's concern, compassion and love for him, then the question is considered artificial and is for showing off. At times a person may ask this question but his heart is filled with rancour (*hiqd*) and resentment (*dighn*), which cause him to be interested in hearing that the person is not in a good state. To be saved from all that, solitude is the solution that enables a person to avoid this. This is because if a person mixes with people and does not adopt their manners they will hate him, find him annoying, backbite him, he will be preoccupied with vengeance and this will affect him in his worldly and religious affairs.

Fourth, one can be influenced with the negative traits of people, as this is a latent illness which the intelligent people are not aware of, let alone the heedless ones. This is because if a person mixes with an immoral person for some time, even if he internally (*bāṭin*) disproves of him, he will find that after some time his aversion from evil will have decreased, because if a person is frequently exposed to evil, he will find it non-repulsive. He will no longer feel the effect and enormity of evil. If a person is always observing others who commit major sins he will belittle the minor sins that he commits.

Similarly, if a person examines the condition of the predecessors in asceticism (*zuhd*) and worship (*ta'abbad*), he will look down upon himself, and he will have a low opinion of his acts of worship. This will spur him to exert himself in the worship of Allāh. These facts show the intent of the person who said, "When the righteous people are mentioned blessings descend."

Among the things which demonstrate if a thing is constantly encountered and seen, that when most people see a Muslim who has not fasted in Ramaḍān, they will almost regard such a person to be a disbeliever. In contrary, these Muslims may see a person who prays after the prescribed time yet they will not be as much repulsed from him as they are repulsed by a person who does not fast at the prescribed time, despite the fact that missing one prayer (for no valid reason) takes a person out of the fold of Islām.[6] There is no other reason for that notion except that prayer occurs frequently and many people are negligent in it. Similarly if a jurist wears a silk garment or a gold ring, people will disprove of him severely. However, if they may see him backbiting people they will not consider that to be a major thing, despite the fact that backbiting is more serious than wearing silk. Nevertheless, due to the fact that people hear others backbiting people many times, and they see backbiters, the effect of backbiting has disappeared from their hearts. Therefore, it is important that you realize these issues and beware of associating with people, because what you will see in people is what will mostly lead you to be greed (*ḥirs*) on acquiring worldly things, heedless (*ghafla*) of the Afterlife, disregarding sins, and weakening your desire (*raghba*) to engage in acts

[6] [Editor's Note] There is a detailed discussion from the scholars about this issue. In short a person who misses prayer and regards that to be permitted goes out of the fold of Islām, and whoever leaves prayer because of laziness does not become a disbeliever, even though, some hadīth have termed such a person a disbeliever. However, this is the disbelief of actions. This opinion is based on reconciling the evidences.

of worship. Therefore, if you find a gathering where Allāh is mentioned do not leave it because it is the spoils (*ghanīma*) of a believer.

The third benefit: Deliverance (*khalāṣ*) from temptations (*fitan*) and disputes (*khaṣūmāt*), and safeguarding religion by not engaging in those things, because cities are rarely free of bigotry (*'aṣabiya*) and disputes excluding a person who isolates himself, he is obviously protected from them.

Ibn 'Umar (*raḍiy-Allāh 'anhumā*) narrated that the Prophet (ﷺ) mentioned about afflictions, described them and said: "When the people will break their promises, betray their trusts, and they will differ while they were previously together like this,"—and he interlaced his fingers." I said: 'What should I do if such a time comes to pass?' The Prophet (ﷺ) said: "Keep to your house, control your tongue, accept what you approve, and abandon what you disapprove, attend to your own affairs, and leave alone the affairs of the common people."[7]

Similar ḥadīths have also been narrated.

The fourth benefit: Being safe from the evil (*sharr*) of people, because at different times they will offend you by backbiting (*ghība*), tale-bearing (*namīma*), thinking ill (*sū' al-ẓann*) of you, and giving you false ambitions (*aṭmā' al-kādhiba*). Whoever mixes with people will most likely encounter jealous people (*ḥāsid*), enemies (*'aduw*) and other types of evil that a person comes across from the people whom he knows. Solitude enables a person to avoid all that. A poet said:

[7] The ḥadīth was transmitted by Bukhārī in his Saḥīḥ but he did not relate its isnād of narrators, vol.1, pp.468. Al-Ḥāfiẓ said: 'This hadīth was transmitted with its isnād of narrators by Ibrāhīm al-Ḥarbī in *Gharīb al-Ḥadīth*.' The ḥadīth was transmitted by Aḥmad #6508, Ibn Mājah #3957 and its isnād of narrators is saḥīḥ.

"Your enemies are from your friends therefore do not have many friends.
Indeed diseases mostly emanate from food or drink."

Ibrāhīm Ibn Adham said, 'Do not introduce yourself to those whom you do not know, and ignore those whom you know.'

A person asked his brother: 'Should I accompany you for *ḥajj*?' He said: 'Let us be content in that Allāh has hidden our faults. Indeed I fear that (if we travel together) we will see in each other what will cause us to hate each other.'

This is another benefit in solitude, and that is Allāh's screening (*sitr*) of a person's faults in religion, propriety, and other shortcomings will continue.

The fifth benefit: That people will lose interest in you and you will lose interest in them. Since pleasing them is an unreachable goal (*ghāya*), thus a person who isolates himself from people will make them lose interest in his attending of their banquets, marriages and so on.

It was said: 'Whoever avoids all the people, they will all like him.'

As for your losing interest; indeed a person who looks at the worldly adornments will be keen to acquire them. His greed for the world will receive impulse by his keenness, and he will be disappointed (khaiba) by not being able acquire most of his desires, thus he will be hurt by that.

A ḥadīth states: "Look at one who is lower than you, and do not look at one who is above you. For indeed that is more worthy that you not belittle Allāh's favors upon you. "[8]

[8] Bukhārī, vol.11, pp.276, Muslim #2963 and Tirmidhī #2515.

Allāh the Exalted said:

وَلَا
تَمُدَّنَّ عَيْنَيْكَ إِلَىٰ مَا مَتَّعْنَا بِهِۦٓ أَزْوَٰجًا مِّنْهُمْ زَهْرَةَ ٱلْحَيَوٰةِ ٱلدُّنْيَا

> "And do not extend your eyes toward that by which We have given enjoyment to [some] categories of them, [its being but] the splendor of worldly life."
>
> [*TāHā* (20): 131]

The sixth benefit: Avoiding mixing with annoying and foolish people, and enduring their behavior. If a person is offended by annoying people, he will start to backbite them. If they criticize him, he will respond in the same manner, and this will cause corruption (*fāsad*) in religion. In solitude there is safety (*salāma*) from that.

Section Two:

On the Pitfalls of Seclusion

Know that there are religious and worldly goals which are acquired by seeking help from others, and that does not happen except through mixing with people.

The benefits of mixing with people include learning, teaching, benefiting others and benefiting from them, disciplining himself and other people, seeking to find pleasure in the company of others and giving them pleasure by accompanying them, friendliness, attaining great reward through fulfilling the rights of others, being accustomed to humbleness, gaining experience through seeing these conditions, and taking lessons from them. These are the lessons of mixing with people.

I will now discuss them in detail:

The first benefit: Learning (*ta'allum*) and teaching (*ta'līm*); I have mentioned the virtues of these things in the chapter of knowledge. A person who has learnt the obligatory religious knowledge and knows that he cannot become an expert in religious knowledge and wants to dedicate himself to the worship of Allāh should seclude himself. If he can be a distinguished scholar of religion then he secludes himself before learning, he will have suffered a great loss.

This is why al-Rabī' Ibn Khuthaym said: 'First learn, then seclude yourself. Knowledge is the basis of religion, and there is no goodness in laymen who seclude themselves.'

One scholar was asked: 'What do you say about an ignorant person who secludes himself?' He said: "That is crazy and void.' He was asked: 'What about a scholar who secludes himself?' He quoted the ḥadīth which states: 'You have no concern with it as it has its water reservoir and feet and it will reach water and drink and eat trees. Leave it till its owner finds it."[9]

As for learning; it entails a great reward (*thawāb 'aẓīm*) for a person who learns with the correct intention (*niyya*). However, if a person's intention (*qaṣd*) is to acquire prestige (*jāh*) and have many followers, then in that there is the destruction of religion. I have mentioned this in the chapter of knowledge. These days most students have the wrong intention for learning religious knowledge, thus religion obligates that they [students] should be avoided. However, if a person happens to come across someone who is learning for the sake of Allāh and seeking nearness to Him, then it is not permissible to be

[9] In the footnotes of the Levite edition of the book, it was stated, "He compared the seclusion of a scholar to a camel which has its feet and water reservoir with it. He meant that the camel can walk, traverse distances, can go to water sources and drink from there, eat from the trees, defend itself from animals which may attack it. This was compared to a person who can walk and has food on a journey. This is similarly to solitude by a scholar because his knowledge safeguards him from the devil and the evil promptings of his own self.

secluded from such a person, and it is unlawful to hide knowledge. A person should not be misled by the statement of the one who said, 'We sought knowledge not for the sake of Allāh, but the knowledge could only be acquired for the sake of Allāh,' because the person meant this statement the sciences of the Qur'ān, ḥadīth, knowledge of the biographies of the Prophets and the Companions. All of that includes threats (*takwīf*) and warnings (*tahdhīr*), and that causes rekindling of the fear (*kawf*) of Allāh in a person's life, and if this knowledge does not cause an impact immediately, it will do so later on. However, the knowledge of scholastic theology (*'ilm al-kalām*) and the sciences of disputation (*'ilm al-khilāf*), does not make the seeker (*rāghib*) of the worldly adornments turn to Allāh, rather a person who studies these sciences will continue being desirous of immersing in them even if he reaches an advanced age.[11]

The second benefit: Benefiting others and benefiting from them (*nafa'a wa'l-intifā'*).

As for benefiting from people; it is through earning a livelihood and transacting. One in need of this is obliged to abandon solitude. However, it is better for a person who has what he is content with to seclude himself, except if he wishes to give away his extra income in charity, then it would be better for him to mix with people and to earn than to remain secluded. However, if based on foresight (*baṣīra*) and not invalid delusions (*awhām*) and imaginations (*khayālāt*), the person sees that seclusion is beneficial for him in recognizing Allāh and getting pleasure (*uns*) in worshipping Him, then he should engage in it instead of mixing with people to seek extra sustenance.

[11] This is the undoubted truth with regards to scholastic theology. However, this is not apply in general to the science of disputation. Where scholars differ in opinion, the evidences should be examined and the preponderant opinion should be chosen based on a good intention and clean heart. Scholars should have the choice to agree to disagree.

As for benefiting people; it is better for a person to benefit people either with his wealth or physical strength to fulfill their needs. If he can undertake this task within the limits of the Sharīʿah, then that is better than seclusion for him if his seclusion is limited to optional prayers (*nawāfil*) and physical action of worship only. However, if he is a person who has been guided to the actions of the heart (*qalb*) like constant remembrance (*dhikr*) and contemplation (*fikr*), then he should never desist from such actions.

The third benefit: Disciplining (*ta'dīb*) and good manners (*ta'addub*); I mean training oneself by enduring mixing with people, striving (*mujāhada*) to bear their annoyance, curbing the soul (*kasr al-nafs*), overcoming desire (*qahr al-shahwa*), and that is better than solitude with respect to a person who has not refined his manners (*akhlāq*).

It should be understood that training (*riyāḍah*) oneself is not for its sake, just like this is not the goal of training an animal. Rather, the aim of training an animal is to use it as a conveyance for travelling over distance. Similarly, the body is a mount which is used to travel on the road to the Afterlife, and it has desires which if not tamed will be difficult for the rider to control on the way. Thus, the person who spends his whole life training himself will be like a person who spent his whole life training an animal but did not ride it, and he does not benefit except by being safe from being bitten or kicked by it. Indeed, that is a benefit, but it is not the main goal.

A monk was called: 'O monk!' He said: 'I am not a monk but I am a voracious dog. I have detained myself so that I do not bite people.'

This is good with respect to a person who offends people but it should be limited to only him.

As for disciplining others; a person will know the latent faults of people when he disciplines them and his state will be like the person who spreads knowledge as has been mentioned.

The fourth benefit: Seeking to find pleasure in the company of others and giving them pleasure by accompanying them; that could be a good thing like seeking pleasure in the company of pious people. This could also be a means of cheering up the heart (*tarwīḥ al-qalūb*) and making it forget the torment of loneliness (*karb al-waḥda*). Therefore, sometimes a person may seek pleasure in the company of someone who does not spoil the rest of his day. A person should strive to talk of religious affairs when he meets people.

The fifth benefit: Acquiring reward and making others acquire it.

As for acquiring reward; that is through attending funerals, visiting the sick, being present at weddings, and invitations. There is reward in this which is attained through making a Muslim happy.

As for making others attain rewards; this is when a person welcomes people to his house so that they may console him, congratulate him or visit him when he is sick. People will earn rewards by this. The same applies if he is a scholar and he permits people to visit him. However, a person should compare the rewards of these types of mixing with people with the negative effects, and based on that he should prefer either solitude or mixing with people. Many of the predecessors used to prefer solitude to these things.

The sixth benefit: Humbleness (*tawāḍi'*); and that cannot be attained in solitude, because pride (*kibr*) may be the reason why a person chooses solitude. He may not go to gatherings because the people do not give him sufficient respect or do not introduce him in a manner that is suitable for his status. He may also avoid mixing with people because his status is higher than theirs, and so on.

A sign of this quality is that a person wants others to visit him but he does not want to visit others. He is happy when the rulers and the common men draw closer to him, and gather at his house and kiss his hand. Choosing solitude because of this is ignorance (*jahl*) because humbleness does not affect the person of high status.

Having known the benefits and pitfalls of solitude, it has been established that giving a detailed general answer in approval or disapproval of it is wrong. However, the person, his condition, the condition of the person who mixes with him, the reason for mixing, the benefits that are lost through mixing, and these lost benefits, should be compared with acquired benefits. At that point the truth will be clear and what is better will be apparent.

Imām al-Shāfiʿī said: 'Being reserved to people causes their enmity (*ʿadāwa*), and opening up to them causes annoyance, thus be moderate in your dealings with people.'

A person who mentions anything besides this will have stated inadequate information. He will be speaking of his condition, and it is not permissible for him to give a ruling for others who are different from him based on his condition.

Section Three:
Etiquettes of Solitude

If it is asked: 'What are the etiquettes of solitude?' I will answer: 'A person engaged in solitude should intend to keep away from harming people, seek safety from the misdeeds of the evil doers, avoid the fault of not fulfilling the rights of the Muslims, and have a dedicated firm purpose in the worship of Allāh. These are clear etiquettes.

In his time alone, a person should be regular in applying his knowledge and engaging in acts of worship, constantly remembering Allāh and contemplating. Thus he will harvest the fruits of solitude. He should prohibit people from coming to him and visiting him, so that he may have free time. He should not ask about the affairs of people, nor listen to the rumors of the area, and what people are doing, because all what is implanted in the heart comes out during prayer. The implantation of news in the ears is like the implantation of seeds in the ground. A solitary person should be content with a simple lifestyle, otherwise wanting a luxurious life will compel him to mix with people.

He should be patient (*ṣabūr*) with the annoyance that he encounters from people. He must not listen when people praise him about his solitude or when they criticize him for not mixing with people, because that affects the heart and will make him to stop from travelling on the road to the Afterlife.

He should have a good companion whom he relaxes with for some time to take a break from the exertion of constant worship, because this will help him in regaining strength for worshipping Allāh. Patience (*ṣabr*) in solitude cannot be attained except by abandoning the hope of attaining (*tam'a*) the worldly things. His hope for worldly things cannot be abandoned except by not having high hopes for a long life. When he wakes up in the morning he should realize that he could die before the evening, and when he reaches the evening, he should realize that he could die before the morning. In this manner, it will be easy for him to be patient because he will be dealing with one day at a time.

He should constantly remember death (*mawt*), and the loneliness of the grave (*qabr*). Whenever his heart is saddened by loneliness, he should be certain that if his remembrance and knowledge of Allāh did not produce in his heart what comforts him, then he will not be able to deal with loneliness after death, and that if a person is comforted by the remembrance and knowledge of Allāh, death will not remove that, because death does not remove the source of comfort and knowledge, as Allāh stated with regards to the martyrs:

بَلْ أَحْيَآءٌ عِندَ رَبِّهِمْ يُرْزَقُونَ ﴿١٦٩﴾

"Rather, they are alive with their Lord, receiving provision."
[*Āl-'Imrān* (3): 169].

Everyone who is dedicated to Allāh in fighting his own self is a martyr, as was stated by one Companions who said: 'We have come back from the smaller *jihād* to the greater *jihād*.'[11]

[11] The isnād of narrators for this report is not authentic as was stated in detail by Shaykh Muḥammad Amān al-Jāmi in *al-Muhadarah al-Difa'iyyah 'an al-Sunnah al-Muhammadiyyah*. It should be pointed out that the common people interpret the great jihād to mean provision for the children, and this is invalid. It is said: "They mean the *jihad* of the self."

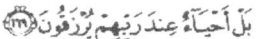

Chapter Seven

On the Ethics in Travelling

Travelling (*safr*) is a means of being saved from what a person is running away from, or reaching that which a person desires.

There are two types of journeys: a physical journey which involves movement away from an area, and the journey of the heart which travels from the lowest of the low places to the dominion of the heavens. This is the more honorable of the two types of journeys. Indeed a person who remains on the condition that he was in after birth, steadfast on what he learnt by imitating his forefathers, will be in a state of constant deficiency, content with a defective upbringing, and exchanging the vastness of the scope of the heavens and earth with the darkness of a narrow prison.

A poet said:

> I did not see any greater fault in people
> than the fault of the people who are capable of
> achieving great things but do not do so.

However, due to the fact a person who embarks on this journey is in grave danger, its pathways have been obliterated.

The physical journey is of several types. It has benefits and many pitfalls, like solitude and mixing with people, which I have discussed previously.

The benefits emanating from the journey result from the fact that people engage in a journey either because they are fleeing from something or desire to acquire something. Fleeing may be running away from an overwhelming issue in worldly affairs like a plague if it appears in a country, fearing temptation (*fitnah*) and disputes, or the expensive prices.

An overwhelming issue in religion is like a person who has been tested in his country by being given honor, wealth, and having ample means, and these things keep him away from dedication to the worship of Allāh. Then such a person will prefer emigration, obscurity and he will avoid wealth and honor, like a person who is invited to be part a religious innovation (*bid'ah*), or work in an impermissible job, and then he seeks to flee (*firār*) from that.

As for travelling for a required matter; that could be worldly like wealth (*māl*) and honor (*jāh*), or either religious like seeking knowledge of religious issues, seeking to embody religious manners, or witness Allāh's signs on the earth. It has been rarely mentioned that someone has attained religious knowledge from the time of the Companions (*raḍiy-Allāh 'anhum*) up to our times except that he acquired knowledge through travelling, and travelled for the sake of knowledge.

As for wanting to know one's own nature and embodying a good character; that is something important because the road to the Afterlife cannot be travelled except by refining the character (*taḥsīn al-khuluq*) and disciplining (*tahdhīb*) it. Journey is called *safar* (in Arabic) because it shows the manners of a person.

In general a person who is in his own country does not show bad manners (*khabā'ith akhlāq*) because the things that he is used of will be around him. However, if he is exposed to the difficulties and burdens of a journey, is not around the things which he is accustomed to, and is afflicted with the trials of being far away from one's country, he will show his bad side, and his defects (*ghawā'il*) will be known.

There are benefits for the intelligent person who sees Allāh's signs on His earth:

There are different parts of land on earth which lie next to each other, and contain mountains, land, deserts, seas, different types of animals and plants. Everything indicates the Oneness of Allāh (*waḥdaniyya*), is hymning the praises of Allāh with an eloquent tongue, and no one realizes this except the one who listens and is heedful.

By listening I mean internal listening, through which a person realizes the pronunciation of the tongue of the state (i.e., the condition of a thing indicates that it is praising Allāh, even if it is not doing that physically by the tongue). There is no atom in the heavens and earth but that it has several signs which indicate the Oneness of Allāh the Exalted.

I have mentioned that some benefits of travelling include fleeing from being employed in an unlawful position of authority, honor, and being attached (*'alā'iq*) to many other things. This is because devotion to Allāh is not achieved except by a heart which is free from other things besides Allāh. It cannot be imagined that a heart can be free from the important things in the world, and the necessary requirements. However, it can be imagined that these things can be lessened and minimized. People who were attached to a few things were saved, while those who were overburdened by being attached to many things were destroyed. The person who is attached to a few things does not make the world his main concern.

Section One:
On Permissible Travelling

One type of journey is the permissible (*mubaḥ*) journey, like travelling for sight-seeing and a picnic. As for random travelling which does not involve a specific destination, or a known place, then that is forbidden.

A ḥadīth transmitted by Ṭāwūs states that the Prophet (ﷺ) said, "There is no monasticism (*rahbāniyya*), and nor hermitage and nor travel by wandering ascetics (*siyāḥah*) in Islām."[1]

Imām Aḥmad ibn Hanbal said, 'There is no travel by wandering ascetics (*siyāḥah*) in Islām and was not practiced by the Prophets and righteous people.'

Due to the fact that a journey distracts the heart, a person seeking to travel should not do so except for seeking knowledge, or visiting a scholar whose *sirah* is exemplary.

[1] The isnād of narrators in this ḥadīth does reach the Prophet (ﷺ). It was transmitted in this manner by 'Abdu'l-Razzāq #15860. However, the ḥadīth was transmitted with a ṣaḥīḥ isnād of narrators by al-Dārimī, vol.2, pp.133 from the hadīths of Sa'd ibn Abi Waqqāṣ who narrated that the Prophet (ﷺ) said to 'Uthmān ibn Maz'ūn, "O 'Uthmān! I was not commanded to practice monasticism. The hadīth was transmitted by Aḥmad with another wording, vol.6, pp.226. It was transmitted by Bukhārī, vol.5, pp.101, Muslim #1202 with the word "*celibacy*". Refer to *al-Durr al-Manthur*, vol.6, pp.177-178, Suyūṭī, and *al-Silsilah al-Ṣaḥīḥah* by al-Albānī, vol.4, pp.378.

The etiquettes of travelling are known which are mentioned in the books which discuss the rites of *ḥajj* and other chapters.

Among the etiquettes is that a person should begin by restoring people's rights, repaying debts, preparing the expenditure for the people whom it is compulsory for him to spend on, and returning things which people have entrusted him with.

Also among the etiquettes is that he should select a righteous companion (*rafīq ṣāliḥ*) for the journey, and bid farewell to his family and friends.

Also among the etiquettes is that the person intending to travel should perform *ṣalāt al-ʿistikhārah*, and he should set out on early on a Thursday.

Additional etiquettes are that he should not travel alone, and that the major part of his journey should be at night. He should not neglect to say the *adhkār* (words uttered in the remembrance of Allāh) as well as supplications, when he arrives at a place, ascends high ground, or descends into a valley.

Other etiquettes are: that he should take with him things which are beneficial to him like the *miswāk*, comb, mirror, kohl jar, and so on.[2]

[2] A ḥadīth about this issue was transmitted, and al-Ḥāfiẓ al-ʿIrāqī said about it in *al-Mughni*, vol.2, pp.256, "The ḥadīth was transmitted by Ṭabārani in *al-Awsaṭ*, al-Bayhaqī in his *Sunan*, al-Khārʾiṭī in *Makārim al-Akhlāq*, and all the paths of the ḥadīth are weak."

Section Two:
On what the Traveller must do

The traveller must take provisions for the world and the Afterlife. As for the provision of the world; it is food and drink and the things which he needs.

He should not say: "I will go out while putting trust in Allāh, and will not take provisions with me," because taking provisions does not contradict trust (*tawakkul*) in Allāh.

As for the provision of the Afterlife; it is the knowledge which he needs for knowing his purification (*tahāra*), prayer (*salāh*), learning the concessions of journeys like shortening prayers, combining prayers (*jam'*), not fasting (*fitr*), knowing the period of time on a journey in which it is permissible to wipe over the socks (*khuffayn*), *tayammum*, voluntary prayers that are made by a person who is on a journey. All these issues and their conditions are mentioned in the books of *fiqh*.

A traveller should know the things which change because of travelling, and that is knowing the direction of the qiblah and the times of prayer, because that is more emphasized on journeys than when a person is at home.

He should seek to know the direction of the *qiblah* by observing the stars, the sun, the moon, the winds, water, mountains, and galaxies, as is explained in the books which deal with the issue. The mountains are considered because all of them face the *qiblah*.

As for galaxies; they are seen in the early part of the night on the left shoulder of the person who is praying, in the direction of the *qiblah*, then the head of the galaxy twists, so that in the last part of the night it will be on the right shoulder of the person who is praying. The galaxies are called the saddles of the sky.

It is imperative to know the times of prayers. The time of Ẓuhr starts when the sun passes the meridian. The traveller should erect a straight stick on the ground, and he should mark the point of the shadow on the stick, and look at it. When he sees the shadow declining, he should know that the time for Ẓuhr has not started. If the shadow is increasing, the traveller should know that the sun has passed the meridian, and the time for Ẓuhr has started, and that is the early part of the time for Ẓuhr. The last part of that time is when the shadow of a thing has become equal to it in length, then the early part of the time for 'Aṣr begins. The end of this time is when the shadow of a thing is twice its length.

It has been narrated that Imām Aḥmad said: 'The time for 'Aṣr exists as long as the sun does not become yellow. If the sun becomes yellow the preferred time for 'Aṣr would have expired and what remains will be the time of necessity until sunset. The rest of the times are known.'

Chapter Eight

On the Ethics of Enjoining Good and Forbidding Evil

Know that enjoining good and forbidding evil (*al-amr bi'l-ma'rūf wa'l-nahyi 'an'l-munkar*) is a major thing (*qutb al-a'ẓam*) in religion, and it is the task which the Prophets were sent to accomplish. If it was abolished, religion would be destroyed, corruption (*fāsad*) would appear and the lands would be destroyed.

Allāh the Exalted said:

وَلْتَكُن مِّنكُمْ أُمَّةٌ يَدْعُونَ إِلَى الْخَيْرِ وَيَأْمُرُونَ بِالْمَعْرُوفِ
وَيَنْهَوْنَ عَنِ الْمُنكَرِ ۚ وَأُولَٰئِكَ هُمُ الْمُفْلِحُونَ ﴿١٠٤﴾

> "And let there be [arising] from you a nation inviting to [all that is] good, enjoining what is right and forbidding what is wrong, and those will be the successful"
>
> [*Āl-'Imrān* (3): 104].

This ayah indicates this duty is a communal obligation (*farḍ 'ayn*) and not an individual obligation (*farḍ kafāya*), because Allāh said:

وَلْتَكُن مِّنكُمْ أُمَّةٌ

"And let there be [arising] from you."

whereas He did not say: "All of you should enjoin what is right."

Therefore if a sufficient number of people engage in this duty, the obligation falls away from the rest of the people. In this ayah success is limited to the people engaged in this duty. There are many verses in the Noble Qur'ān concerning enjoining what is right and forbidding what is wrong.

Al-Nu'mān ibn Bashīr (*raḍiy-Allāh 'anhu*) narrated: 'I heard the Messenger of Allāh (ﷺ) saying: "The example of the person abiding by Allāh's order and restrictions in comparison to those who violate them is like the example of those persons who drew lots for their seats in a boat. Some of them got seats in the upper deck, and the others in the lower deck. When the latter needed water, they had to go up to bring water (and that troubled the others), so they said, Let us make a hole in our share of the ship (and get water) saving those who are above us from troubling them. So, if the people in the upper part left the others do what they had suggested, all the people of the ship would be destroyed, but if they prevented them, both parties would be safe."'[1]

[1] Bukhārī, vol.6, pp.58, Tirmidhī, vol.6, pp.295, Aḥmad, vol.4, pp.268,269,270.272, Abū'l-Shaykh in *al-Amthāl*, p.317 and al-Ramahurmuzi in *al-Amthāl*, pp.103-104

Section One:
On the Stages of Enjoining Good and Forbidding Evil

It has been transmitted in a well-known ḥadīth from the narrations of Imām Muslim that the Prophet (ﷺ) said: "Whoever amongst you sees an evil, he must change it with his hand (*yad*); if he is unable to do so, then with his tongue (*lisān*); and if he is unable to do so, then with his heart (*qalb*); and that is the weakest form of faith (*iḍ'af al-īmān*)."[2]

Another ḥadīth states, "The best *jihād* [in the path of Allāh] is (to speak) a word of truth to an oppressive ruler (*sultān jā'ir*)."[3]

Another ḥadīth sates, "If you see my *ummah* being afraid of telling an oppressor, "You are an oppressor, then (know that) Allāh has forsaken them."[4]

And it is related that Abū Bakr al-Ṣiddīq (*raḍiy-Allāh 'anhu*) said in a sermon that he delivered: 'O people, you are reading this verse:

يَٰٓأَيُّهَا ٱلَّذِينَ ءَامَنُوا۟ عَلَيْكُمْ أَنفُسَكُمْ
لَا يَضُرُّكُم مَّن ضَلَّ إِذَا ٱهْتَدَيْتُمْ إِلَى ٱللَّهِ مَرْجِعُكُمْ جَمِيعًا

"O you who are believers, you watch for yourselves. No

[2] Muslim #49, Tirmidhī #2173, Abū Dāwūd #1140 and #4340, and Nasā'ī, vol.8, pp.111 from the ḥadīths of Abū Sa'īd (*raḍiy-Allāh 'anhu*).

[3] Abu Dāwūd #4322, Tirmidhī #2265, Ibn Mājah #4011, Aḥmad, vol.3, pp.19, al-Ḥumaydī #752, Ḥākim, vol.4, pp.505 and al-Qaḍā'ī #1286 from the ḥadīth of Abū Sa'īd (*raḍiy-Allāh 'anhu*).

[4] Aḥmad, vol.2, pp.163, 189-190, 191, al-Bazzār in his *Zawaid* #2033, Ṭabarānī, Ḥākim, al-Bayhaqī in *al-Shu'b* from the ḥadīth of Ibn 'Umar (*raḍiy-Allāh 'anhu*). There is a break in the isnād of narrators of this ḥadīth. It was transmitted by Ṭabarānī in *al-Awsat* from the ḥadīth of Jābir (*raḍiy-Allāh 'anhu*). Sayf Ibn Hārūn is one of the narrators of the ḥadīth, and he is a weak narrator. In *Fayḍ al-Qadir*, vol.1, pp.354), al-Manāwī attributed the ḥadīth to Tirmidhī, and I did not see it there.

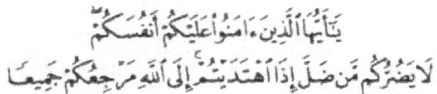

> harm shall befall you from one who is misguided once you have been guided."
>
> [*al-Mā'idah* (5): 105]

And I have heard the Messenger of Allāh (ﷺ) saying: "There are no people who are disobedient and fail to repent while having living among them a rightly guided person, but that Allāh is about to engulf them in a punishment from Him."[5]

Section Two:

On the Pillars, Conditions, Levels and Etiquettes on Enjoining Good and Forbidding Evil

Know that there are four pillars on enjoining good and forbidding evil:

Firstly, the enjoiner (*munkir*) must be a legally responsible Muslim who is capable of enjoining good. This is the condition for the compulsoriness (*wujūb*) of enjoining what is right.

A discerning boy may enjoin good, and he will be rewarded for that. However, it is not compulsory upon him to command people to do good.

Some scholars said that the person involved in enjoining others to do what is good must be morally upright. They state, "An immoral person (*fāsiq*) may not enjoin people to do what is good. They supported this opinion with Allāh's statement:

أَتَأْمُرُونَ ٱلنَّاسَ بِٱلْبِرِّ وَتَنسَوْنَ أَنفُسَكُمْ

> "Do you enjoin right conduct on the people, and forget (To practice it) yourselves?"

[5] Tirmidhī #3059, #2169, Abū Dāwūd #4322, Ibn Mājah #4005, Aḥmad, vol.1, pp.16, 29,30, 59, Ibn Ḥibbān #1837, al-Marūzī in *Musnad Abū Bakr* #86, 87 and 88 and its isnād is ṣaḥīḥ.

[*al-Baqarah* (2): 44].

However, that is not a strong proof.

On the other hand, some scholars made it conditional that the enjoiner should have the permission to engage in the task from the ruler (*imām*) or his representative (*wālī*), and they did not allow individuals to engage in this duty on their own. This opinion is invalid because the verses and general ḥadīths indicate that whoever sees an evil deed (*munkar*) committed yet he remained silent, had disobeyed Allāh. Thus specifying (*takhṣīṣ*) the evidences by stating that the ruler has to permit it is absolutism.

It is strange that the Rawāfiḍ had something more to say on this issue: 'It is not permissible to enjoin what is good until the infallible Imām comes out.' These people are the least qualified to talk about the issue.[6] The reply to their claims is that when they come to a judge (*qāḍī*) demanding their rights, they should be told: 'You will attain your rights by the process of enjoining what is right, taking your rights from the oppressors and the time for that has not come because the Imām has not come out yet!'

If it is said, "Enjoining what is right establishes authority over the person who is enjoined, thus it was not established for a disbeliever over a believer, despite the fact that it is a right, therefore it should not be established for individuals without authorization from the ruler.

I will reply: 'As for the disbeliever; he is prohibited from doing that because it consists of power and honor. As for individual Muslims; they deserve this honor through their being Muslims and their knowledge.'

[6] Refer to *al-Washī'ah fī Naqd 'Aqā'id al-Shī'ah* by al-Qāzānī, the edition by the 'Ammār Publishing and Distribution Company Ammān.

Section Three:
The Stages of Guarding against infringements

Know that there are five stages (*marātib*) in guarding against infringements (*hisba*):

The first stage is making it known (*ta'rīf*) that such and such an action is an infringement.

The second stage is admonition in a soft voice (*al-wa'z bi'l-kalām al-latīf*).

The third stage is scolding (*sabb*) and being harsh (*ta'nīf*), and I do not mean that the perpetrator should be scolded in an indecent manner (fāhisha). Rather, we should say to him, "O ignorant person! O foolish person! Do you not fear Allāh?" and so on.

The fourth stage is prevention of evil (*man' bi'l-qahr*), like doing away with musical instruments (*malāhi*)*, and throwing alcohol (*khamr*) away.

The fifth stage is warning (*takwīf*) and threatening to beat (*tahdid bi'l-darb*) the perpetrator, or beating him until he leaves the sin. This stage can be carried out by the Muslim leader (*imām*), contrary to the previous stages, because it could lead to civil strife and public disorder.

The fact that the pious predecessors continually kept on enjoining upon the rulers to do what is right and prevent them from what is wrong, is a clear proof that they had a consensus in opinion that this

* In *al-Muhalla*, Ibn Hazm said: 'It has been transmitted to us from the most authentic of paths that the companions of Ibn Mas'ūd (*radiy-Allāh 'anhu*) used to meet the slave girls in the streets and tear the drums that these girls carried.'

task did not need the ruler's permission.

If it said: 'Does a child, a servant, wife and subject have the right to enjoin upon his father, husband and the ruler to do good, and prohibit him from what is evil?'

I will respond: 'Everyone has the right to enjoin good and prohibit what is evil, and I have stated that guarding against infringements comprises of five stages.'

Within these stages the child can accomplish two stages; state that such and such a thing is evil as well as admonish (*wa'ẓ*) and counsel in a soft voice (*nuṣḥ bi'l-luṭf*).

He is also allowed to act upon the fifth stage; he may do away with the lute (a musical instrument), throw away alcohol, and so on. This order is also applicable to the servant and wife.

As for the subjects and the ruler; the issue is more serious than that of a child and his father. Thus a person can only tell the ruler that such and such a thing is evil and he can counsel him (and he is not able to proceed to other stages which are above that).

It is conditional that the enjoiner of good should be able (*qādir*) to enjoin what is right. As for the incapable person (*'ājiẓ*); he should not enjoin what is right except in his heart (*qalb*). The obligation to enjoin good does not fall away because of tangible inability (*'ajẓ al-ḥissī*), rather, fear (*kawf*) of an undesirable thing that may afflict a person as a result of enjoining good, is considered to be inability.

Similarly, if a person knows that his prohibition of what is evil will not be beneficial; his situation will be of four types:

Firstly, if he knows that the evil will be removed because of his statements or action, and he will not be harmed, then it is compulsory for him to forbid evil.

Secondly, if he knows that his statements will not be beneficial, rather, if he speaks he will be beaten; then in this case it will not be compulsory for him to forbid evil.

Thirdly, if he knows that his forbidding of evil will not be beneficial, however, he does not fear any harm either, then in this case it will not be compulsory for him to forbid what is evil because it will be of no use. However, it is recommended for him to engage in this action as a means of publicizing Islāmic rites and reminding people of the religion.

Fourthly, if he knows that he will be harmed if he forbids evil but evil will be invalidated by his action like if he breaks the lute (a musical instrument like guitar), throws away alcohol, but he knows that he will be beaten after that; then it will not be compulsory for him to do so. However, forbidding of evil will be recommended in this case because of the ḥadīth which states, "The best *jihād* [in the path of Allāh] is (to speak) a word of truth to an oppressive ruler (*sultān jā'ir*)."

There is no difference of opinion among the scholars that it is permitted for a single Muslim to attack the lines of the disbelievers and fight, even if he knows that he will be killed. However, if he knows that he will not have an effect on the disbelievers like a blind man who throws himself into the lines of the disbelievers, then it is prohibited for him to do that. Similarly, if a Muslim sees alone immoral person who has a cup of alcohol and a sword in his hands, and he knows that if criticizes him, he will still drink the alcohol and strike his neck with a sword, then it will not be permissible for him to criticize him, because his forbidding of evil in this case does not have a positive effect. Rather, it is recommended for a person to prohibit evil if he can invalidate the evil deed, and his action is beneficial.

If he knows that he will be beaten together with his friends, then it will not be permissible for him to guard against infringements, because he is incapable of preventing evil except through means which lead to another form of evil. That is not classed as ability at all. In this discussion "knowing" means to know with high probability (*galaba al-zann*), thus if a person deems it highly probable that he will be harmed, then it is not compulsory for him to enjoin what is good, and if he deems it highly probable that he will not be harmed, then it will be compulsory for him to forbid evil. In this issue, the condition of the coward will not be considered, nor will the state of the person who is reckless in his bravery. Rather, the state that is considered is that of a person who has a moderate temperament (*mu'tadil al-tab'*), sound disposition (*salim al-muzāj*). By harm, I mean being beaten, being killed, being a victim of looting, being publicized and being given a bad reputation. As for being insulted and sworn at; these are not excuses for not forbidding evil, because a person who enjoins what is right mostly encounters that.

The second pillar: The issue which is being prohibited should be a forbidden thing which is currently present and manifest. To be a forbidden thing means that its occurrence should be forbidden in the Sharī'ah. A forbidden thing is more general than a sin, because whoever sees a small boy or a mad person drinking beer should throw the beer away and forbid him from doing that. Similarly, if a person sees a mad man committing adultery with a mad woman or an animal, he must forbid him from that.

My statement *'currently present'*, excludes a person who has drunk alcohol and finished doing so, and so on, because such an issue is not for individuals. Additionally, this statement excludes what will happen later, like if it is known from contextual evidence that a person intends to drink alcohol at night. In this case, no prohibition occurs except through admonishing the person.

My statement '*manifest*', excludes a person who commits a sin but shields himself in his house, or closes the door to his house. In this case, it is not permissible to spy on the person, except if the sin that he commits can be detected by people outside his house, like the sound of musical instruments and lutes. A person who hears such sounds may enter the house and break the musical instruments. Likewise, if the smell of beer emanates from a certain place, the preponderant opinion is that people should go to the site and forbid this sin.

For forbidding an evil deed, it is conditional that it should be known that the action is an evil deed without *ijtihād* (independent reasoning/judgment). Thus there is no prohibition for an issue which is subject to *ijtihād*. Therefore, a Ḥanafī should not criticize a Shāfiʿī for eating an animal which has been slaughtered without mentioning Allāh's name. Similarly, a Shāfiʿī should not criticize a Ḥanafī for drinking a small quantity of *nabith*[8] which is not intoxicating.[9]

The third pillar: concerns the one being prohibited. Everyone must be prohibited from committing evil, and it is not stipulated that he should be legally responsible as I have previously explained that small boys and mad people must be prevented from evil.

The fourth pillar: concerns with guarding against infringements, and this has stages and etiquettes:

[8] A drink made by mashing up dates and letting the juice sit for three days. What you got was *nabith*, a sweet tasting and mildly fermented beverage

[9] This is not a general issue according to the Ḥanafīs. For a detailed discussion on this refer to *al-Radd al-ʿIlmi*.

The first stage: The person prohibiting the evil deed should see it being committed before prohibition. Therefore, he is not permitted to eavesdrop on another person's house in order to hear the sound of musical instruments. Similarly, he should not smell a person so as to detect the smell of alcohol on him. He should not touch what is covered by a garment so as to know the shape of a musical instrument. He should not request for information from his neighbours in order to know what has happened. However, if two morally upright Muslims inform him that so and so is drinking alcohol, he should enter the perpetrator's house and prevent this.

The second stage: People should be told about evil actions, because the ignorant engage in deeds which they do not consider to be unlawful. However, when they know that these actions are impermissible they stop doing them. An ignorant person should be told: "A person is not born as a scholar. Indeed, we were ignorant in the matters of the Sharī'ah until the scholars taught us. Maybe there are no scholars in your village." This is required so that the ignorant person is taught about the evil deed without being offended. Whoever does not prohibit an evil action for fear of offending a Muslim, despite the fact that the prohibition is indispensable, is like a person who washes off blood with urine.

The third stage: Prohibition by admonition, advice and telling the person to fear Allāh. The person who is prohibiting evil should quote the ḥadīths which contains warnings (of punishment for wrongdoers), he should tell the perpetrator about the life history of the pious predecessors. This should be done in a gentle manner, without force or anger. There is a major fault which should be avoided, and that is when a scholar prohibits evil and thinks that he is honorable because of his knowledge, and considers the ignorant person to be disgraceful because of his ignorance.

This scenario is similar to a person who saves others from the fire while burning himself in it. This attitude is the highest degree of ignorance (*jahl*), a great disgrace, and self-conceit (*ghurūr*) from the devil. There is a benchmark and standard for (knowing and avoiding) this, and it is that the person prohibiting a perpetrator from evil wishes that someone else had done so. If preventing evil is difficult and cumbersome for him, and he wishes that someone else could do the task, then he should prohibit evil, because his motive is religious. If the opposite is true, then he is following his own desires, and seeking to show his honor through prohibiting evil. Therefore, he should fear Allāh and begin by prohibiting himself from evil.

Dāwūd al-Ṭā'i was asked: 'What do you think of a person who goes to the rulers and enjoins them to do good and prohibits them from evil?' He said: 'I fear that he will be whipped.' He was told: 'He can bear that.' He said: 'I fear that he will be killed by a sword.' He was told: 'He can bear that.' He said: 'I fear for him the latent illness; self-conceit (*'ujb*).'

The fourth stage: Scolding and rebuking with rough words. This stage is resorted to when soft words do not have the required effect, and the perpetrator shows persistence, mocks the admonition and counsel. By scolding, I do not mean using coarse speech (*fahsh*) and lying (*khadhbib*). Rather, we should say to the perpetrator, "O immoral person! O fool! O ignorant person! Do you not fear Allāh?" Allāh the Exalted states that Ibrāhīm told his people:

أُفٍّ لَّكُمْ وَلِمَا تَعْبُدُونَ مِن دُونِ اللَّهِ أَفَلَا تَعْقِلُونَ

> "Fie upon you, and upon that which you worship besides Allāh! Have you then no sense?"
>
> [*al-Anbiyā'* (21): 67].

The fifth stage: Physically stopping the evil deed like breaking musical instruments, throwing away alcohol, and removing a person from a house that he has usurped. There are two etiquettes for this stage:

First, the person prohibiting evil should not resort to physical means if the perpetrator already responds to verbal commands. Thus if he tells him to vacate from the usurped house, he readily goes out then in that instance he should not pull him or push him.

Second, he should break the musical instruments in a manner which invalidates their use, and should not exceed that. When throwing away alcohol, he should avoid breaking the utensils, as much as possible. If he has no choice but to stone the containers of alcohol (to break them) then he may do so. He will not be liable for the value of the containers. If a perpetrator covers alcohol with his hands, the person prohibiting evil may hit his hands so that he can get access to the alcohol and throw it away. If the alcohol is in bottles which have thin mouths, such that if it would require much time and the immoral people may come to him while he is doing so and prevent him from that, then he may break the glasses, because this is an acceptable excuse (for destroying property). Similarly, if throwing away the alcohol will waste time, and prevent him from doing his work, then he should break the bottles, even if he is not afraid that the immoral people will disturb him.

If it is asked: 'Is it not permitted to break the bottles, and to pull a person away from a usurped house as a deterrent?'

My response is: 'That is permissible for the authorities, and is not permissible for individual people, because this is an issue of *ijtihād*.'

The sixth stage: Threatening and warning like saying: "Leave this or else I will do this and that to you." Where possible this should be done first before discipling a person.

The etiquette (*adab*) in this stage is that a person should not threaten a perpetrator with an illegal threat like if he says: "I will loot your house," or "I will capture your wife and make her my slave," because such statements contain the resolve to engage in unlawful actions and that is prohibited. If he utters these statements with no resolve to do them, then he is lying.

The seventh stage: Discipling a person using hands and feet in a manner which does not involve threatening him with a weapon. This is permissible for individuals provided that it is limited to need and necessity, and when the perpetrator stops the evil action, the discipling should also stop.

The eight stage: At times a person cannot stop the evil action himself, and needs the help of others who will threaten the perpetrator. However, the immoral person may also seek the help of his allies.

The correct view in this situation is that this issue needs the ruler's permission because it leads to civil strife and turmoil.**

** Editor's Note: Matters of this nature need to be referred to a higher authority such as government agencies that look after the affairs of the people. Every land has a system and rules, and those should be adhered to. It is not permitted to take law into your own hands.

Section Four:
On the qualities of the person engaged in preventing infringements

I have mentioned the etiquettes of the person engaged in preventing infringements. I have summarized the qualities of such a person as follows:

1. Knowledge (*'ilm*) of the status of infringement (*hisbah*), its definition and where it is enacted.

2. Fear of Allāh (*wara'*), because a person may know something and not act according to it due to some reason.

3. Good manners (*husn al-khuluq*), and that is essential because it enables a person to desist from committing evil, because if a person's anger (*ghadab*) is aroused, then knowledge and fear of Allāh alone will not be sufficient in suppressing it if the person is not endowed with good manners.

One of the predecessors said: 'None should enjoin good except a person who is gentle (*rafiq*) in enjoining, gentle in prohibiting evil, patient (*halīm*) in enjoining good, patient in prohibiting evil, knowledgeable (*faqih*) of what he is enjoining, and knowledgeable of what he is prohibiting.'

Other etiquettes include: limiting (*taqlīl*) links to people, and giving up hope (*tam'a*) of benefiting from them, so that a person will not have to resort to cajolery. It has been stated that one of the righteous predecessors had a cat, and everyday he would get some meat from the butcher who was his neighbour. Thereafter, he saw the butcher engaged in some evil deed. He then put the cat out of his house. He went to the butcher and prohibited him from his deed. The butcher said: 'From today, I will not give you anything for the cat.' He said: 'I did not prohibit you except after I had taken the cat away from my house, so that I will not need anything from you.'

This is correct (*ṣaḥīḥ*), because if a person relies on people for two things, he will not be able to prohibit them from evil, and these things are:

Firstly, because of the things which they provide him with, he is unable to fulfill this noble act.

Secondly, he fails to do this due to pleasing them and being praised by them.

It is compulsory to be gentle in enjoining good and prohibiting evil. Allāh the Exalted said:

فَقُولَا لَهُۥ قَوْلًا لَّيِّنًا

"And speak to him with gentle speech (*qawl al-layin*)."
[*Ṭāhā* (20): 44].

A narration states that Abū'l-Dardā' (*raḍiyAllāh 'anhu*) passed by a man who had committed a sin and was being scolded by the people. He said: 'What if you had found him in a well; would you have taken him out?' They said: 'Yes, we would have taken him out.' He said: 'Therefore, do not scold your brother, and praise Allāh who has saved you from what the perpetrator did.' They said: 'Do you not hate him?' He said: 'I hate his actions, and if he leaves them, he is my brother.'

A boy was passing through a road dragging his garment behind him (i.e., the length of his garment reached below his ankles). The companions of Ṣilah ibn Ushaym wanted to rebuke him severely. He said: 'Let me suffice for you in his issue.' Then he said: 'O my brother's son! I need something from you.' The boy said: 'What is it?' He said: 'I want you to lift your garment.' He said: 'Yes, I will please you by obeying you.' He then lifted his garment. Ṣilah told his companions: 'This is better than what you wanted to do, because if you had scolded him and offended him, he would have also insulted you.'

Al-Ḥasan was invited to a wedding. A container made of silver which had sweets made from dates and fat was brought to him. He took the sweets, and put them on a loaf of bread, and then from there. A person said, "This is silent prohibition (of an evil deed)."

Chapter Nine

On the Reprehensible Actions, which people are accustomed to, and enjoining rulers to do good and forbidding them from doing evil

I will divide this chapter into two sections as follows:

Section One: Reprehensible Actions

Know that the reprehensible actions (*munkarāt*) which people are accustomed to cannot be enumerated. However, I will point out some sins which are an indication of the rest.

[i] The reprehensible actions of the masajids

Some of which are witnessed many times in the masajids include not observing tranquility (*tamāniyya*) in *rukū'* and *sujūd*, and all the things which affect the correctness of prayer (*siḥa al-ṣalāh*) like impurities (*najāsa*) which are on a worshipper's clothes but he does not see them, and facing away (*inḥirāf*) from the qiblah due to blindness or darkness.

And mistakes (*al-laḥn*) in the recitation (*qirā'a*) of the Qur'ān. It is better for a person who is in the state of *i'tikāf* to be engaged in criticizing these things and tell people about them than for him to engage in voluntary acts of worships (*nāfila*) which benefit him only.

Also reprehensible actions include: the muezzins making the adhān with one voice and elongating the madds of the words.

Other include: wearing of silk clothes by the sermon-giver (*khāṭib*), or holding of a golden sword in his hands.

Additional reprehensible actions include what the story-tellers do in the masajids like lying and prohibited things like talking of things which cause civil strife (*fitan*), and so on.

More include: free intermingling of men and women. People should be prohibited from that.

Additional reprehensible acts include: having gatherings on Friday (*al-Jumm'ah*) for selling medication, food, talismans (*tawīdhāt*), begging, recital of poetry (*ash'ār*), and so on. Some of these things are prohibited (*ḥarām*) while others are detestable (*mukrūh*).

[ii] Reprehensible actions in the markets

These include lying (*kadhib*) about the rate of profit on goods, not disclosing defects (*'ayb*) on goods. Whoever lies and says: 'I bought this item for ten dirhams, and I will get a profit of one dirham on it', is an immoral person.

It is compulsory upon a person who knows of this to inform the buyer of the seller's lying. If he keeps quite because of his consideration for the seller, then he is a partner in cheating (*kiyāna*). Similarly, if a person knows of a defect in a commodity he must tell the buyer about it. Moreover, whoever knows of the occurrence of manipulation in the weighing and measuring of goods should prohibit that, either by himself, or he can tell the authorities to rectify that.

Other reprehensible acts include invalid conditions, engaging in interest (*ribā'*), selling musical instruments (*malābi*), statues (*sūra al-mujassam*)[1] and so on.

[iii] Reprehensible acts in the streets

These include things like building a shop that is attached to buildings that are owned by other people, erecting parts of buildings which protrude into the street, and planting trees if that leads to the constriction of the road and prejudice to the people who pass through the road. However, putting an amount of wood and food that can be carried home by people is permissible, because that is a common need.

Other reprehensible actions include tying an animal on the road in such a manner that the road becomes constricted and this discomforts people. This must be prohibited, except if a person does that out of the need to get down from the animal.

More reprehensible acts include making an animal carry a load

[1] Pictures from things which are not statues are prohibited.

that it is incapable of carrying, throwing rubbish onto the road, throwing water melon peels on the road, or throwing water on the street in a manner which is likely to cause the passersby to slip. This is with regards to water which comes from a specific gutter. If it is rain water, then it is the responsibility of the ruler to deal with the issue, and individuals are not required to do that.

[iv] Reprehensible actions in bathhouses

These include having pictures of animals on the door of the bathhouse or inside. Defacing such a picture is a sufficient way to obliterate it, because this invalidates the picture. If a person cannot prohibit the putting of pictures on a bathhouse, he is not allowed to enter it except in a case of necessity. If his situation is not that of necessity then he should use another bathhouse.

Additional reprehensible actions include uncovering the private parts (*'awrāt*), looking at them, uncovering the thighs for the masseur, and what is below the navel so that he may remove impurity or touch the private parts.

More reprehensible actions include: dipping dirty hands and utensils into a little amount of water. If a Mālikī does that he should not be prohibited. Rather he should be addressed with gentle speech and told: 'You can avoid offending me by not spoiling my means of purification.'

[v] Reprehensible actions in hosting people

These include spreading silk carpets for men, putting incense in a gold or silver censer, using such a container for drinking liquids, using rose water in it, hanging curtains with pictures, listening to

[2] For a detailed discussion on this issue refer to *Ādāb al-Zafāf* by Shaykh al-Albānī.

singing girls[2] and music, and women looking at young men who may tempt them.

It is not reprehensible to have pictures on cushions and carpets. Similarly, silk carpets and gold are permissible for women. No concession has been provided for perforating the ears of young girls[3] to put gold earrings on them, because that causes a painful wound and is impermissible, and having necklaces and bracelets is sufficient. Hiring out these things is impermissible and the money received for that is unlawful.

Other reprehensible acts include hosting an innovator (*mubtadi'*) who speaks about his innovation (*bid'ah*). It is not permissible to attend such gatherings except for a person who can refute (*radd*) the innovator. If the innovator will not speak, it is permissible for a person to attend such gatherings, and display dislike (*karaha*) for the innovator and ignore him. It is not permissible to attend a gathering where a buffoon makes rude (*faḥsh*) jokes and lies (*kadhab*). It is compulsory to prohibit him from that. If a person makes jokes which do not involve lies or obscenity, then that is permissible. However, it is not permissible to be a professional and customary buffoon.

[iv] General reprehensible actions

Whoever is certain that there is a reprehensible action which always goes on in the market, or at a certain time and he is capable of stopping it; the obligation for him to stop this action does not fall away by his staying at home, rather, it is imperative for him to go and stop it. If he can stop part of the evil action then he should do so.

[3] In *Tuḥfah al-Mawlud*, p 209 Ibn Qayyim al-Jawziyyah stated that a narration from Aḥmad permits this.

It is compulsory for every Muslim to start within by reforming himself through being constant in performing the compulsory deeds and avoiding the prohibited things. Then he should teach his family and relatives. After that he should reform his neighbours and the people of his locality, then the people of his country, thereafter he should go to the masses, and the farthest parts of the world. If a person who is nearer to the people reforms them, the obligation to reform falls away from the person who is farther than him. If that is not the case, then every capable person should prohibit evil according to his ability.

Section Two:

Enjoining Rulers and Sultans to do Good and Prohibiting them from doing Evil

I have mentioned the stages of enjoining good and prohibiting evil. It is permissible to apply the first two stages to the sultans which are: informing the sultans that such and such an action is evil and admonishing them. However, addressing the sultan roughly like saying: "O oppressor!", "O person who does not fear Allāh!" is not permissible if it leads to commotion whose consequences may affect third parties. If a person knows that he is the only one who will be afflicted if he utters these words, then he may do so according to the majority of the scholars. However, my view is that this is impermissible because the objective is to prevent evil, and inciting the sultan to deal with him in an unjust manner is greater an evil than that which the person sought to prevent. This is because sultans deserve respect, and if they hear a subject saying to a sultan: "O oppressor!", "O immoral person!" they would consider that to be highly disrespectful and they will not hesitate to attack the person who says that.'

Imām Aḥmad said: 'Do not confront a sultan because his sword is unsheathed. What has been transmitted that the pious predecessors confronted their rulers is because the rulers used to revere the scholars, and when they were relaxed with them, they could bear their criticism in general.'

I have compiled the advices of the pious predecessors to the caliphs and rulers in my book *al-Miṣbāḥ al-Muḍī'*, and I will choose some stories from it and mention them here:

1-Sa'īd ibn 'Āmir told 'Umar ibn al-Khaṭṭāb (*raḍiy-Allāh 'anhu*)[4]: 'I am advising you with some words on the general principles and parameters of Islām: 'Fear Allāh in relation to people, but do not fear people in relation to Allāh. Your actions should not contradict what you say, for the best speech is that which is affirmed by action. Love for all the Muslims that which you love for yourself. Be prepared to face hardship for the truth, and do not be afraid of the blame of the critics (if you do the right thing) in issues which concern Allāh.' 'Umar said: 'Who can do that, O Abu Sa'īd?' He replied: 'A person who has assumed the responsibility that you have assumed.'

2-Qatādah[5] said: 'Umar ibn al-Khaṭṭāb (*raḍiy-Allāh 'anhu*) came out of the masjid with al-Jārūd, and he saw a beautiful woman in the road. He greeted the woman and she replied to his greeting. She said: 'O 'Umar! I saw you while you were young wrestling with other boys in the 'Ukāz market[6]. You quickly grew up, and you attained the position of caliph. Therefore, fear Allāh concerning your subjects, and know that the person who fears death fears that one day he will not be on this earth.' 'Umar (*raḍiy-Allāh 'anhu*) cried. Al-Jārūd said: 'You had the audacity to speak to the caliph in this manner, and you have made him cry.' 'Umar (*raḍiy-Allāh 'anhu*) said: 'Leave her. Don't you

4 *Al-Miṣbāḥ al-Muḍī'*, vol.2, pp.32, *Muḥāḍarah al-Abrār*, vol.2, pp.112.
5 *Al-Miṣbāḥ*, vol.2, pp.37 and *al-'Aqd al-Farīd*, vol.2, pp.358.
6 *Mu'jam al-Buldān*, vol.3, pp.704.

know her? She is Khawla bint Ḥākīm (*raḍiy Allāh ʿanhu*) whom Allāh heard her speak while He was above the seven heavens. So, by Allāh! ʿUmar must listen to her speech.'

3-An old man from the tribe of Azd came to a Muʿāwiyah's chamber and said: 'O Muʿāwiyah! Fear Allāh. Know that each day and night that comes by takes you further away from the world and brings you closer to the Afterlife. Behind you is something that you cannot escape. A flag which you cannot pass has been erected. How quickly will you reach the flag! How soon will the thing coming after you catch up with you! Indeed we and the world perish, but the Afterlife lasts forever. If you do good, you will attain goodness in the Afterlife, and if you act in a bad manner, you will be punished.'

4-Sulaymān Ibn 'Abdu'l-Mālik[7] came to Medīnah and stayed there for three days. Then he said: 'Is there anyone present here who met the Companions, so that he may narrate to me some ḥadīths?' He was told: 'There is a person called Abū Ḥāzim[8] he sent for him, and he came.'

Sulaymān said: 'O Abū Ḥāzim ! Why are you disinclined from me?' Abū Ḥāzim said: 'What disinclination have you seen from me?' He said: 'All the noble people of Medina came to me but you did not come.' He said: 'I do not know you so as to come to you.' He said: 'The Shaykh has spoken the truth. O Abū Ḥāzim! Why do we fear death?' He said: 'Because you are more concerned about the world than the Afterlife, thus you detest transferring from the place that you strived for to the place that you did not strive for.' He said: 'You have spoken the truth. O Abū Ḥāzim ! How will we go to Allāh the Exalted?' He said: 'As for the righteous person; he will go to Allāh like an absent person who returns and meets his family while he is

[7] *Al-Miṣbāḥ*, vol.2, pp.48 and *Hilyah al-Awliyā'*, vol.3, pp.234.
[8] Salamah ibn Dīnār, he died in 140H. His life history is mentioned in *al-Tahdhīb*, vol.4, pp.143.

happy, and the evil person will go to Allāh like a runaway slave who goes back to his master in a sad and fearful state. Sulaymān cried and said: 'O Abū Ḥāzim would that we knew what our reward with Allāh will be.' Abū Ḥāzim said: 'Judge yourself according to the Qur'ān, and you will know your status with Allāh.' He said: 'How will I get such knowledge from Allāh's book?' He said: 'In Allāh's statement:

إِنَّ ٱلْأَبْرَارَ لَفِي نَعِيمٍ ﴿١٣﴾ وَإِنَّ ٱلْفُجَّارَ لَفِي جَحِيمٍ ﴿١٤﴾

"Indeed, the righteous will be in pleasure. And indeed, the wicked will be in Hellfire"

[*al-Infiṭār*: 13-14].

He said: 'O Abū Ḥāzim , where is the mercy of Allāh?' He said:

قَرِيبٌ مِّنَ ٱلْمُحْسِنِينَ ﴿٥٦﴾

"Near those who do good"

[*al-A'rāf*: 56].

He said: 'O Abū Ḥāzim ! Who is the most intelligent person?' He said: 'The one who learns wisdom and teaches it to people.' He said: 'Who is the most foolish person?' He said: 'Whoever puts himself at the disposal of an unjust people, and sold his Afterlife for the worldly life.' He said: 'O Abū Ḥāzim ! What is the supplication that is answered the most?' He said: 'The supplication of those who fear Allāh and humble themselves before him.' He asked: 'What is the most pure charity?' He said: 'The one given by a person with insufficient means.'

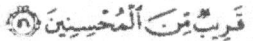

He said: 'O Abū Ḥāzim ! What do you say about our situation? He said: 'Let me not talk about that.' Sulaymān said: 'It is advice that you will be giving.' He said: 'Some people acquired power forcefully without consulting the Muslims, nor acting on the consensus of the opinion of the people. They spilt blood in order to acquire worldly gain, then they left the world. Would it be that I knew what they said, and what said to them? Some of the people in the gathering said: 'What an evil thing you have said: 'O Shaykh!' Abū Ḥāzim said: 'You have lied. Allāh took a covenant from the scholars that they should clarify knowledge and not hide it.' Sulaymān said: 'O Abū Ḥāzim! Accompany us and we will benefit each other.' He said: 'I seek refuge in Allāh from that.' He said: 'Why?' Abū Ḥāzim said: 'I am afraid that I will be slightly inclined to you and Allāh will punish me. He said, 'Advice me.' He said: 'Fear Allāh and do not let Him see you where he has prohibited you from being at, and do not let find him find you absent from a place that he has commanded you to be.'

He said: 'O Abū Ḥāzim! Make a good supplication for me.' He said: 'O Allāh! If Sulaymān is your friend, make goodness easy for him, and if that is not the case guide him to the truth. Sulaymān said: 'O boy! Give me one hundred dinars". Then he said: 'Take it, O Abū Ḥāzim!' He said: 'I do not need this money. I and others have an equal right in this wealth. If you give us equally then I will accept, otherwise I do not need it. I fear that what I have told you will apply to me if I accept the money. Sulaymān seemed impressed by Abū Ḥāzim and al-Ẓuhrī said: 'He is my neighbour for the past thirty years and I have never spoken to him.' Abū Ḥāzim said: 'You forgot Allāh and then forgot me.' Al-Ẓuhrī said: 'Are you scolding me?' Sulaymān said: 'Rather, you have scolded yourself. Do you not know that a neighbor has a right over his neighbour?' Abū Ḥāzim said: 'When the children of Israel were on the right path the rulers needed the scholars, but the scholars used to flee from them because they wanted to safeguard their religion. Thus, when some lowly people noticed that they sought knowledge and came with that to the rulers. So, the people joined each other in doing evil. They failed and they relapsed. If the scholars safeguarded their religion and knowledge, the rulers would have continued respecting them. Al-Ẓuhrī said: 'It is as if you mean me and you are talking indirectly.' He said: 'The issue is as you are hearing.'

5-It was stated that a Bedouin came to Sulaymān ibn 'Abdu'l-Mālik, and he said: 'O commander of the faithful! I am going to say some words to you, so bear them even if you do not like them because the words contain goodness, if you accept them. He said: 'Speak.' He said: 'O commander of the faithful! You are surrounded by men who have bought your worldly benefit for their Afterlife, and they have bought your happiness for Allāh's wrath. They feared you in matters concerning Allāh but they did not fear Allāh in matters concerning you. They destroyed their Afterlife and built the world. They are at war with the Afterlife and at peace with the world. Thus, do not entrust them with what Allāh has entrusted you with. They will not care whether they abuse the trust or whether the *ummah* collapses, and you will be responsible for what they committed, and they are not responsible for what you have done. Therefore, do not reform their Afterlife by destroying your Afterlife. Indeed, the person who loses the most is he who sells his Afterlife for someone else's worldly riches. Sulaymān said: 'You have let your tongue loose and it is more devastating than your sword.' He said: 'Yes, O Commander of the faithful! These words are for you and not against you.' He said: 'Do you need anything?' He said: 'I do not have a specific need which excludes all the others.' Then he stood up and went. Sulaymān said: 'What a good man he is, how honorable is his lineage, how steady is his heart, how eloquent is he! How sincere is his intention! How good he is! How fearful of Allāh he is! This is how honor and intellect should be like.

6- 'Umar Ibn 'Abdu'l-'Azīz[9] said to Abū Ḥāzim : 'Advice me.' He said: 'Lie down, and imagine that you are at the point of death, and consider the state that you would like to be in at that time, and now

[9] *Al-Miṣbāḥ*, vol.2, pp.80 and *Ḥilyah al-Awliya'*, vol.5, pp.317.

start doing actions which will make you attain that state. Similarly, consider the state that you detest to be in at that point and now leave the actions that will lead to that state.

7- Muḥammad ibn Ka'b[10] told 'Umar ibn 'Abdu'l-'Azīz: 'O Commander of the faithful! The world is a market, people get from it what harms them and benefits them. How many people were deceived by what is similar to what we are experiencing, till death came to them, and they left the world as sinners and did not have the preparation for Paradise where they wanted to go, nor did they have protection against the Fire which they wanted to avoid. People who did not praise them divided their estates among themselves, and the deceased went to the One who will not excuse them. O Commander of the faithful! We must consider their enviable good actions and follow them in doing them, and we must consider their [evil] actions which we fear that they will be punished for and avoid them. Therefore, fear Allāh! Open your doors to the people. Be easily accessible, help the oppressed, and solve the people's grievances. There are three things which if they are in a person, he will have complete faith in Allāh; if he is happy, his happiness does not lead him to commit invalid acts, and if he is angry, his anger does not cause him to act unjustly, and if he has authority he does not take what is not his.

8- 'Aṭā ibn Abī Rabāḥ went to Hishām. He welcomed him and said: 'What do you need O Abū Muḥammad!' He had with him some noble people who were talking, they became silent. 'Aṭā reminded Hishām about the provisions and grants for the people of Makkah and Madīnah. He said: 'Yes, O boy! Make arrangements for the people of Makkah and Madīnah to be granted with their provisions.' Then he said: 'O Abū Muḥammad! Do you have another need?' 'Aṭā said: 'Yes," then he reminded him about the people of Ḥijāz, Najd, and

[10] *Al-Miṣbāḥ*, vol.2, pp.78 and *Sīrah 'Umar ibn 'Abdu'l-'Azīz*, p.134.

the fortified borderline cities. Hishām provided for them like he had provided for the people of Makkah and Madīnah. He then advised him not to demand from the dhimmis more than they could bear. He agreed to that. After that Hishām said: 'Is there any other need?' 'Aṭā said: 'O Commander of the faithful! Fear Allāh. Indeed you were created alone, you will die alone, you will be resurrected alone, and you will be judge alone. By Allāh, you will not be with these people whom you are seeing.'

He said (i.e., the narrator): 'Then Hishām began to cry. 'Aṭā stood up and left the place. When he was at the door, a man followed him and gave him a bag which we do not know whether it contained dirhams or dinar. The man said: 'The Commander of the faithful ordered me to give you this.' 'Aṭā said:

وَمَآ أَسۡـَٔلُكُمۡ عَلَيۡهِ مِنۡ أَجۡرٍۖ إِنۡ أَجۡرِيَ إِلَّا عَلَىٰ رَبِّ ٱلۡعَٰلَمِينَ ١٢٧

"And I do not ask you for it any payment. My payment is only from the Lord of the worlds."

[*al-Shu'arā'* (26): 127].

Then he went out and by Allāh he did not drink a single drop of water there.'

9- Muḥammad ibn 'Alī[11] narrated: 'I was sitting in the gathering of Manṣūr, and ibn Abī Dhi'b was also present who was the governor of Madinah during the time of Al-Ḥasan ibn Zayd. People from the Ghifār tribe came to Abū Ja'far al-Manṣūr and complained about Al-Ḥasan ibn Zayd. Al-Ḥasan said: 'O Commander of the faithful! Ask ibn Abi Dhi'b about them.' He said: 'He asked him about them.' He said: 'I testify that they are a people who attack the honor of others.' Abū Ja'far said: 'You have heard.' The Ghifāris said: 'O Commander

[11] *Al-Misbāḥ*, vol.1, pp.402 and *Muḥāḍarah al-Abrār*, vol.1, pp.463.

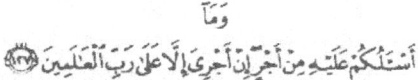

of the faithful! Ask him about Al-Ḥasan ibn Zayd. He asked him. He said: 'I testify that he rules unjustly.' Abū Ja'far said: 'You have heard, O ḥasan! He said: 'O Commander of the faithful! Ask him about yourself.' He said: 'What do you say?' He said: 'Will you forgive me O Commander of the faithful! (if I say the truth and offend you?).' He said: 'By Allāh, you will tell me.' He said: 'I testify that you took this wealth unjustly, and gave it to undeserving people.' Then he put his hand on ibn Abi Dhi'b's nape and said: 'By Allāh, had I not controlled myself I would have attacked the Persians, the Romans, the people of Daylam and the Turks. Ibn Abi Dhi'b said: 'Abū Bakr and 'Umar were leaders and they took wealth justly and distributed it fairly, and they attacked the Persians and the Romans. Abū Ja'far left him and he said: 'By Allāh were it not for the fact that I know that you are telling the truth I would have killed you.' He said: 'By Allāh, I am more sincere to you than your son al-Mahdi.'

10-Al-Awzā'ī[12] (may Allāh have mercy on him) said: 'Al-Manṣūr sent for me while I was at the coast. I went to him, and when I arrived, I greeted him. He asked me to sit down, and he said: 'What delayed you, O Awzā'ī?' I said: 'What do you want, O Commander of the faithful?' He said: 'I want to learn from you.'

I said: 'O Commander of the faithful! Beware of listening to something and then not following it. Al-Rabī' shouted at me, and he wanted to take his sword. Al-Manṣūr reprimanded him and he said: 'This is a gathering of reward not punishment.' I relaxed and talked freely, then I said: 'O Commander of the faithful! Makḥūl narrated to me from 'Aṭiyyah ibn Busr who said: 'The Messenger of Allāh (ﷺ) said: 'Allāh has prohibited the entry into Paradise of any ruler who dies while he is deceiving his subjects.''[13]

[12] *Al-Misbāh*, vol.2, pp.122 and *Hilyat al-Awliya'*, vol.6, pp.136.

[13] This is an authentic ḥadīth which was transmitted by Bukhārī, vol.13, pp.112 and Muslim #142 on the authority of Ma'qal ibn Yasār (*radiy-Allāh 'anhu*).

"O Commander of the faithful! Previously you were responsible for your own affairs but by becoming caliph you are now responsible for all the people of different colors, the Muslims, and the non-Muslims, and all of them require justice from you. How will be your condition if multitudes upon multitudes of people complain because of difficulties that you caused them or because of your injustice!

O Commander of the faithful! Makḥūl narrated to me from Ziyād ibn Jāriyah from Ḥabīb ibn Maslamah that the Messenger of Allāh (ﷺ) invited a Bedouin to retaliate on him for an unintentional scratch that the Prophet(ﷺ) caused on his body. Then Jibrīl came to him and said: 'O Muḥammad! Indeed Allāh did not send you as a despot nor as a proud person.' The Prophet (ﷺ) called the Bedouin and said: 'Retaliate against me.' The Bedouin said: 'I have forgiven you. May my mother and father be sacrificed for you. I would never do that. Then the Prophet (ﷺ) supplicated for the Bedouin.[14]

O Commander of the faithful! Restrain yourself for your own benefit, and engage in deeds which ensure your safety from the punishment of Allāh.

O Commander of the faithful! If authority was eternal for those who were before you, it would not have reached you. Therefore, authority will not be permanent for you as was the case with your predecessors.

O Commander of the faithful! It has been transmitted in the following verse from your grandfather:

مَالِ
هَٰذَا ٱلْكِتَٰبِ لَا يُغَادِرُ صَغِيرَةً وَلَا كَبِيرَةً إِلَّآ أَحْصَىٰهَا

[14] The isnād of transmitters in the hadīth is not correct.

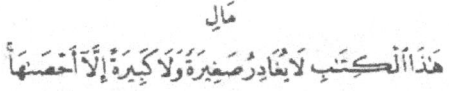

> "What sort of Book is this that leaves neither a small thing nor a big thing."
>
> [*al-Kahf* (18): 49]

that *"a small thing"* means a smile, and *"a big thing"* means laughing. What about what has been done by the hands, and spoken by the tongues?'

O Commander of the faithful! I have been informed that 'Umar ibn al-Khaṭṭāb (*raḍiy-Allāh 'anhu*) said:[15] 'If a lamb was to die on the shores of the Euphrates river because it was lost there, I would be afraid that Allāh will ask me about it. What about a person who has been treated unjustly in your presence?

O Commander of the faithful! It has been transmitted in the following ayah from your grandfather:

يَٰدَاوُۥدُ إِنَّا جَعَلۡنَٰكَ خَلِيفَةٗ فِي ٱلۡأَرۡضِ فَٱحۡكُم بَيۡنَ ٱلنَّاسِ
بِٱلۡحَقِّ وَلَا تَتَّبِعِ ٱلۡهَوَىٰ

> "O Dāwūd, indeed We have made you a successor upon the earth, so judge between the people in truth and do not follow [your own] desire."
>
> [*Ṣād* (38): 26],

that the *ayah* means: when two litigants sit down before you for judgment, and you like one of them, do not wish that he wins the case, because I will take away my prophethood from you, and you will not be my representative. O Dāwūd! The role that I have given my messengers over my worshippers is like that of the camel shepherds because of their knowledge of caring for people, lenient administration, so that they may aid the injured, and guide the weak to sources of food and drink.'

[15] *Ḥilyat al-Awliyā'*, vol.1, pp.53.

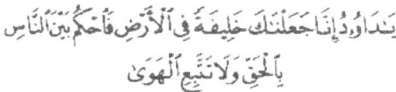

O Commander of the faithful! Indeed you have been tested with a matter which if it was presented to the heavens, earth, and mountains, they would have refused to bear it and would have been afraid of the responsibility.

O Commander of the faithful! Yazīd ibn Yazīd ibn Jābir narrated to me from 'Abdu'l-Raḥmān ibn Abi 'Amrah al-Anṣārī that 'Umar ibn al-Khaṭṭāb (*raḍiy-Allāh 'anhu*) employed a man from the Anṣār to collect charity. After some days he saw that the man was still around and had not travelled. He asked him: 'What prevented you from going to your work?' Do you not know that you will get a reward equal to those who fight in the path of Allāh? He said: 'No.' 'Umar asked him: 'Why?' He said: 'Because I have been informed that the Messenger of Allāh (ﷺ) said: 'Anyone who has authority over the affairs of the Muslims will be brought on the Day of Judgment and his hands will be tied to his neck. He will be made to stand on the bridge of Hell. The bridge will shake him in such a manner that all the organs of his body will be displaced. Then he will taken to account. If he was good, he will be saved because of his goodness, and if he was evil, the bridge will sink him, and he will go down into Hell for a distance which is equivalent to seventy years' travel.'[16]

'Umar said: 'Who did you hear this from?' He said: 'From Abū Dharr and Salmān (*raḍiy-Allāh 'anhuma*)''. 'Umar sent for them, and asked them about the narration. They said: 'Yes, we heard it from the Messenger of Allāh (ﷺ).' Then 'Umar said: 'O 'Umar! Who will bear the responsibility of authority? Abū Dharr (*raḍiy-Allāh 'anhu*) said: 'The one whom Allāh has granted humbleness.'

Then Al-Manṣūr took a cloth, put it on his face, cried and wailed until he made me cry.

[16] The isnād of narrators given by Abū Nu'aym for the story is not correct. However, the narration has been authentically transmitted by others.

Then I said: 'O Commander of the faithful! Your grandfather al-'Abbās asked the Messenger of Allāh (ﷺ) to appoint him as the governor of Makkah, Taif or Yemen. Then the Prophet (ﷺ) said: 'O uncle! It is better for you to save yourself (from the Fire) than to have a position of leadership which you may not fulfill its rights.'[17] He did this because he wanted to advise his uncle and he had sympathy for him. When the verse:

وَأَنذِرْ عَشِيرَتَكَ ٱلْأَقْرَبِينَ ﴿٢١٤﴾

"And warn, [O Muḥammad], your closest kindred."
[*al-Shu'ara'* (26): 214]

was revealed, the Prophet (ﷺ) told his uncle that he could not avail him at all against Allāh, and he said: 'O 'Abbās! O Fāṭimah! I will not avail you at against Allāh. I have my actions and you have your actions.'[18]

'Umar ibn al-Khaṭṭāb (*raḍiy-Allāh 'anhu*) said: 'The affairs of people are only administered well by a judicious person, who does not fear criticism concerning issues to do with Allāh. He then advised al-Manṣūr more and said: 'This is the advice. *Assalamu 'Alaykum.*'

He stood up and said: 'Where are you going.' He said: 'I am going home with the permission of the Commander of the faithful. He said: 'I have permitted you to go, I thank you for your advice, and I have accepted it, and Allāh is the Granter of success and He helps people to acquire it. I seek His help, I depend on him, He is sufficient for me and He is the best disposer of affairs. Do not hesitate to give

[17] In *al-Mughni*, Al-Ḥāfiẓ al-'Irāqī said: "The ḥadīth was transmitted by Ibn Abi Dunya with a broken isnād of transmitters. The ḥadīth was also transmitted by al-Bayhaqī from the ḥadīth of Jābir (*raḍiy-Allāh 'anhu*) with an isnād of narrators which reach the Prophet (ﷺ). He also transmitted it with a broken link of narrators from ibn al-Munkadir. Then he said, "The ḥadīth is known as a mursal ḥadīth ."

[18] Bukhārī, vol.8, pp.386, Muslim #206, Tirmidhī #3184, vol.6, pp.248 from the ḥadīth of Abū Hurayrah (*raḍiy-Allāh 'anhu*).

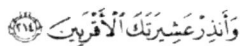

me similar advices (in the future). Indeed your word is acceptable, and your advice is not blameworthy.'

He said: 'I will do that *Inshā'Allāh.*'

He ordered him to be given money to help him with his travelling expenses but he did not accept it. He said: 'I do not need it. I will not sell my advice for all the worldly things.' Al-Manṣūr then became aware of his view and he could not respond to that.

11- When al-Rashīd[19] went for *ḥajj*, he was told: 'O commander of the faithful! Shaybān has come for *ḥajj*. He said: 'Look for him and bring him to me.' Shaybān was brought, and al-Rashīd said: 'O Shaybān, advice me! He said: 'O Commander of the believers! I stammer and I am not fluent in Arabic. Therefore, bring a person who understands what I say. A person who could understand his speech was brought. He addressed the person in the Nabatieh language (an old language that was spoken in 'Irāq), and said: 'Tell him that the person who warns you before you reach a place of safety gives you better advice than the one who gives you reassurance before you reach a fearful place. Al-Rashīd said: 'What is the interpretation of this?' He said: 'Tell him that the person who tells you, 'Fear Allāh because you are responsible for this *ummah*, and Allāh has entrusted you over it, given you authority over it, and you are responsible over it, so be fair to the subjects, divide wealth justly, send warriors to fight in Allāh's cause, and fear Allāh; is the person who has warned you that when you reach the place of safety you will be safe. Such a person is better for you than the one who says that you are from a family which has been forgiven, you are the relatives of the Prophet and he will intercede for you. Such a person will keep on reassuring you such that when you reach a fearful situation you will be destroyed."' He said: 'Then Hārūn cried to such an extent that those who were around him felt sorry for him.' Then he said: 'Give me more advice.'

[19] *Al-Miṣbāḥ*, vol.2, pp.183 and *Ṣifah al-Ṣafwah*, vol.4, pp.340.

He said: 'What I have told you is sufficient for you.'

12-'Alqamah ibn Marthad[20] said: 'When 'Umar ibn Habīrah came to 'Irāq, he sent for Al-Ḥasan and al-Sha'bī. He ordered them to stay in a house and they were there for approximately one month. Then he came to them, sat down and showed them respect. He said, 'Indeed the Commander of the faithful Yazīd ibn 'Abdu'l-Mālik has written a letter to me. However, if I carry out his commands I will be destroyed. If I obey him I would have disobeyed Allāh, and if I disobey him, I would have obeyed Allāh. Do you think that there will be a way out for me if I follow his orders?' Al-Ḥasan said, 'O Abu 'Amr, answer the Amir.' Al-Sha'bī spoke and made light of ibn Habeerah's situation and it seemed that he was giving him justification to follow the orders. He said, 'What do you say O Abu Sa'īd?' He said, 'O Amir, al-Sha'bī has said what you have heard.' He said, 'What do you say?' He replied, 'I say, O 'Umar ibn Habīrah! Soon two of Allāh's angels who are unfriendly and rough, who do not disobey what Allāh commands them will come down to you and take you away from the vastness of your palace and take you to the narrowness of your grave.'

'O 'Umar ibn Habīrah! If you fear Allāh, He will save you from Yazīd ibn 'Abdu'l-Mālik, and Yazīd ibn 'Abdu'l-Mālik will never save you from Allāh.'

'O 'Umar ibn Habīrah! Do not feel reassured for Allāh may see you in the worst state while you are obeying Yazīd ibn 'Abdu'l-Mālik, and He will close the doors of forgiveness for you.'

'O 'Umar ibn Habīrah! I met people from the early part of this *ummah*, and they used to flee from the world when it was being opened

[20] *Al-Miṣbāḥ*, vol.2, pp.211 and *Ḥilyat al-Awliyā'*, vol.2, pp.149.

up for them more than you seek it while it is fleeing from you.'

'O 'Umar ibn Habīrah! I fear for you a situation which Allāh the Exalted warned you against, when He said:

ذَٰلِكَ لِمَنْ خَافَ مَقَامِي وَخَافَ وَعِيدِ ﴿١٤﴾

> "This is for him who fears standing before Me (on the Day of Resurrection) and also fears My Threat."
>
> [*Ibrāhīm* (14): 14]'

'O 'Umar ibn Habīrah! If you fear Allāh, he will suffice for you against Yazīd ibn 'Abdu'l Mālik, and if you follow Yazīd ibn 'Abdu'l-Mālik in disobeying Allāh, He will leave you to his devices.'

'Umar ibn Habīrah cried, and he stood up while tears were flowing from his ears.

The following day he sent for them to grant them permission to leave and to reward them. He gave more to Al-Ḥasan than to al-Sha'bī. Al-Sha'bī went out to the masjid and said, 'O people! Whoever can give preference to Allāh over his creation, let him do so. By Him in Whose hands is my soul, Al-Ḥasan does not know anything which I am not aware of but I wanted to please ibn Habīrah but Allāh drove me away from him.'"

13- Muḥammad ibn Wāsi'[21] (may Allāh have mercy on him) came to Bilāl Abi Burdah on a hot day while Bilāl was in a shelter made of sackcloth, and he had ice. He asked him: 'O Abū 'Abdullāh! What do you think of my house?' He said: 'Indeed your house is good, but Paradise is better than it. Remembering the Fire makes one forgetful of your house. He asked him: 'What do you say about status?' He said: 'Your neighbours are the inhabitants of the graves. Think of them, for they have no need for status.' He said: 'Make supplications

[21] *Al-Misbah*, vol.2, pp.207 and *Akhbār al-Quḍāh*, vol.2, pp.52.

to Allāh for me.' He said: 'What will you do with my supplication, and there are people in such and such a place who are saying that you oppressed them. Their supplications will be lifted before mine. Do not oppress anyone, and you will not need my supplication.'

This is a summary of the narrations in connection with the advices of the pious predecessors to the rulers. Whoever wants to know more about that let him read *al-Miṣbāḥ al-Muḍī'*.

This was the conduct of the scholars and their custom in enjoining good, prohibiting evil, while disregarding the authority of the sultans in this matter, and their preference of establishing Allāh's rights to fearing them. However, the sultans knew the right of knowledge and its virtues and they were patient when they heard the stern advices by the scholars. In contrast, in these times, my view is that fleeing from the sultans is better, because the rulers of these days, even if they respect meetings with scholars, they are only satisfied with gentle words and advice. This is due to two reasons:

One of the reasons is associated with the adviser, and that is his bad intention, and his inclination towards the world and showing off. Therefore, he will not be sincere in his advice.

The second reason is linked with the person who is being advised because the love of the world has distracted the people from remembering the Afterlife, and their reverence of the world has made them forget the reverence of the scholars, and a believer should not disgrace himself.

This is the end of the book of enjoining good and prohibiting evil. Before that the author had written a book on listening to singing and ecstasy. I will briefly mention some things from it.

Chapter Ten

On the Ruling of Listening to Music, Singing, and Dancing

Know that listening (*samā'*) to singing (*ghinā'*) is one of the major ways in which the devil (*iblīs*) gets into corrupt people's hearts. He has deceived an uncountable number of scholars (*'ulamā'*) and ascetics (*zuhhād*), let alone the laymen, till they claimed that they concentrate on Allāh's worship when they hear melodious songs. They thought that listening to songs results in a form of enjoyment (*tarb*) in the hearts and ecstasy (*wajd*) is linked to the Afterlife.

If you want to know the truth, look at the first century of Islām. Did the Prophet (ﷺ) or his companions do such? Then look at the sayings of the generation following that of the Companions (*tābi'ūn*), and the generation following them (*tab' tābi'ūn*), and the scholars of this nation like Imām Mālik, Imām Abū Ḥanīfah, Imām al-Shāfi'ī, and Imām Aḥmad (may Allāh have mercy on them). All these people criticized singing, to such an extent that Imām Mālik said: 'If a person buys a slave girl and discovers that she is a singer, then he should return her.' He was asked about singing, and he said: 'It is done by the immoral people (*fussāq*).'

Imām Aḥmad was asked about a man who died and left behind a child and singing slave girl, and the boy needed to sell her. He said: 'She is sold based on the fact that she is a simpleton and not a singer.' He was told: 'Her value is thirty thousand dinārs if she is a singer, and if she is sold on the basis that she is a simpleton her value will be twenty dinārs. He said: 'She should not be sold except on the basis that she is a simpleton.'

The scholars have (successively) criticized singing. From the latter day scholars Abū'l-Ṭayyib al-Ṭabarī[1] who was one of the greatest Shāfi'ī Scholars wrote a book[2] on the issue, in which he was severe in his prohibition of singing. Some people who have been tested in their faith are the ones who are attached to singing and they said: 'It was allowed by some of the salaf.'

Imām Aḥmad ibn Ḥanbal heard a poet reciting some verses and he said: 'There is no problem with this.'

Thus we should ponder on what was allowed by Imām Aḥmad. He allowed the poems on asceticism (*ash'ār al-zuhadiyya*) and poems of the similar kind, which do not involve striking sticks (*ḍarb bi-qaḍīb*), or musical instruments (*ālat al-ṭarib*), nor are they combined with clapping (*tasfiq*) and dancing (*raqṣ*).

This is how the ḥadīth of 'Ā'ishah (*raḍiy-Allāh 'anhā*) concerning the two singing girls who sang about what the Anṣār said during the battle of Bu'āth[3], should be interpreted, because that does not cause a person to be exultant.

[1] He died in 450H. His life history is mentioned in *Ṭabaqāt al-Shafi'yyah*, vol.3, pp.176.
[2] There is a manuscript of the book in *al-Rabāṭ* and it is entitled *Jawāb fi'l-Sama' wa'l-Ghina'*
[3] Bukhārī, vol.2, pp.366, Muslim #892 and Nasā'ī, vol.3, pp.195.

It is known that the earlier Muslims did not have what the latter Muslims have invented in the form of the tambourine (*daff*), castanet (*ṣanj*), flute (*shabbāba*) and romantic poetry (*shi'r al-raqīq*), because these things incite latent passions (*hawa al-kāmin*) in people, disturb them, and the ignorant (*jāhil*) will think that this disturbance (*inzi'āj*) is linked to the Afterlife but it is far from it.

It would have been better if they had stated, "This is a permissible (*mubāḥ*) type of amusement (*lahw*), and we are comfortable with it." However, they think that listening to singing is an act of worship, and they call the exultation which results in from singing and makes them lose their senses (*'aql*) as ecstasy (*wajd*). Sometimes ecstasy may lead to impermissible things like tearing clothes, and confusion. All these things are contrary to the way of the salaf.

It is clear that this is misguidance (*ḍalāl*). Thus, a person must not mislead himself because the correct ecstasy (*wajd al-ṣaḥīḥ*) is the ecstasy of the heart (*wajd al-qalb*) when it listens to the Qur'ān and sermons which allow the fear (*kawf*) of warnings (*wa'īd*), the longing (*shawq*) in promises (*wa'd*) and resentment on inadequacy impulse the inner self have not been insufficient in order to attain concentration, will desire to attain what Allāh has promised, and regret (*nadm*) over negligence (*tafriṭ*). A combination of these internal issues (*ḥarakāt al-bāṭina*) necessitates calmness of the exterior (*sukūn al-ẓāhir*), not jumping (*jamz*), and clapping (*taṣfīq*). The Qur'ān, religious exhortations, sermons, poetry on asceticism (*zuhd*) have not been insufficient in order to attain concentration on Allāh, that uselessly we need to mention 'Salmā and Sa'dāh'. I do not deny that some of those poems may coincidentally cause the heart to be attached to the Afterlife but most of them make the heart to be inclined to the worldly desires instead.

The example of a person who wants to use singing to benefit in the

Afterlife is like one who says, "I will look at a handsome beardless youth so that I may be pleased with the creation of the Almighty"; such a person is wrong because things which incite desire and are liked by a person's nature when they are looked at disturb thinking and prevent it happening. Therefore, we will prohibit such a person from doing so and say to him, "Look at things which do not disturb you."

Allāh said:

أَفَلَمْ يَنظُرُوٓا۟ إِلَى ٱلسَّمَآءِ فَوْقَهُمْ كَيْفَ بَنَيْنَٰهَا وَزَيَّنَّٰهَا

> "Have they not looked at the heaven above them, how We structured it and adorned it"
>
> [*Qāf* (50): 6].

If a person says: I am not affected by what impacts others in the form of being naturally drawn to desires, then he is claiming something which is contrary to the natural disposition (*jibla*), and his claim must not be considered. I have discussed this at length in my book entitled *Talbīs Iblīs*[4], thus, I have not discussed the issue in detail here. And Allāh knows best.

[4] A lengthy discussion on Music and Singing pp331-379. Complete translation of the classical text available in English under the title, 'The Devil's Deceptions' by Imām Ibn Jawzī published by Dār as-Sunnah Publishers 2014.

Chapter Eleven

The Conduct of Life as Exemplified by the Prophet's Character

Know that the external manners (*ādāb al-ẓawāhir*) are an indication of internal manners (*ādāb al-bawāṭin*), the movement of the limbs (*ḥarakāt al-jawāriḥ*) are the fruits of thoughts (*thamarāt al-khawāṭir*), actions (*a'māl*) are the results of manners (*natā'ij al-akhlāq*), etiquettes (*ādāb*) are best part of knowledge (*rash al-ma'ārif*), the secrets of the hearts (*sarā'ir al-qulūb*) are the sources (*manābi'*) and seeds of actions (*maghāris al-a'māl*) and the lights of the secrets (*anwār al-sarā'ir*) are the ones that make the exterior shine, decorate it and adorn it.

If a person's heart (*qalb*) is not fearful of Allāh, his limbs will not be fearful,[1] and if a person's heart (*ṣadr*) is not a lantern of Godly light (*mishka al-anwār al-ilāhiyya*), then his exterior will not be illuminated by the beauty of the prophetic character (*jamāl al-ādāb al-nabuwiyya*).

---

[1] This issue is divided into sections. Refer to the epistle *al-Khushū' fī'l-Ṣalāh* by Al-Ḥāfiẓ ibn Rajab al-Ḥanbalī. Please refer to the English translation, 'Humility in Prayer' under the Ibn Rajab series published by Dār as-Sunnah Publishers 2007

I have previously mentioned a number of etiquettes, thus, there is no need to repeat them at this point. However, I will suffice by mentioning some etiquettes and manners of the Prophet (ﷺ) so that we will combine the etiquettes with the importance of knowing the noble manners (*akhlāq al-karīma*) of the Prophet (ﷺ). A single action of the Prophet (ﷺ) is a sufficient testimony that he is the most noble of creation (*akram al-khalq*), the highest (*a'lā*) in status (*martaba*), and the most sublime (*ajall*) in ability (*qudra*), so how about a combination of all the manners?

'Ā'ishah (*radiy-Allāh 'anhā*) was asked about the character (*khuluq*) of the Prophet (ﷺ) and she said: 'His character was an embodiment of the Qur'an, he would be angry at the things which the Qur'an prohibited, and he would be happy when the things commanded in the Qur'an were done."[2]

After Allāh perfected the character of the Prophet (ﷺ), he praised him and said:

وَإِنَّكَ لَعَلَىٰ خُلُقٍ عَظِيمٍ ﴿٤﴾

"And indeed, you are of a great moral character"
[*al-Qalam* (68): 5]

Glorified be Allāh, who gave him the Prophet (ﷺ) a noble character and then He praised him.

[2] This hadīth was transmitted with this wording in by al-Bayhaqī in *al-Dalā'il*, vol.1, p.310. Suyūṭī transmitted it in *al-Durr al-Manthūr*, vol.6, p.250, and he attributed it to Ibn al-Mundhir and Ibn Mardawayhi, and both of them transmitted the ḥadīth on the authority of Abū'l-Dardā' (*radiy-Allāhu 'anhu*). The ḥadīth was originally transmitted by Muslim #139, Abū Dāwūd #1342, Ibn Mājah #2333, Ḥākim, vol.2, p.499, Ibn Ḥibbān #466, Aḥmad, vol.6, p.54, 91, 111.

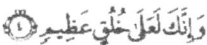

Section One:
A Summary Account of His (ﷺ) Manner and Character

The Prophet (ﷺ) was the most forbearing (*aḥlam*) of people, and also most generous (*askhā*) and the most caring (*a'ṭaf*) of them. He (ﷺ) would mend his own sandals, patch his own clothes and help his family with the daily errands. He (ﷺ) was extremely shy (*ḥayā'*); shyer even than a virgin behind a veil.

He (ﷺ) would respond to the invitation of slaves, visit the sick, walk alone, allow others to ride with him on his mount, accept gifts, eat food that was sent as a gift; though he (ﷺ) never consumed anything that had been given as charity. He (ﷺ) did not have enough dates with which to be satiated, nor was he satiated with barely-bread for more than three consecutive nights.

He (ﷺ) would tie a stone on his stomach to lessen the pangs of hunger. He (ﷺ) would eat whatever food was readily available and never did he criticise food. He (ﷺ) never ate reclining, and ate from what was immediately in front of him.

The most beloved of food to him was meat. The shoulder of a sheep was his favorite. From the legumes, he liked pumpkins, from condiments he liked vinegar, and the most beloved dates to him were the *'ajwah*.

He (ﷺ) would wear whatever he would find. Sometimes he (ﷺ) would wear a lined garment made of cotton which originated from Yemen, and at times he (ﷺ) would wear a cotton *jubbah*.

He (ﷺ) would ride a camel, and at times he would ride a mule, and he (ﷺ) would occasionally ride a donkey and at times he (ﷺ) would walk barefoot.

He (ﷺ) loved perfumes and disliked foul odours. He (ﷺ) honoured people of virtue, and maintained affectionate ties with nobles and dignitaries. He (ﷺ) never snubbed anyone and would accept the excuse of those who presented excuses.

He (ﷺ) would joke, but never would he utter anything untrue. He (ﷺ) laughed, but did not burst with laughter. He (ﷺ) would not let any time pass without being in the service of Allāh, Exalted is He, or being engaged in whatever was essential for his own self-development.

He (ﷺ) never once cursed a woman, nor abused a servant. Never did he strike anyone, except for in *jihād* in Allāh's path. He (ﷺ) did not exact revenge for his own sake, but did so when Allāh's limits had been transgressed. If he (ﷺ) was presented with two options he adopted the easier of the two, unless it entailed disobedience or the severing ties of kinship—in which case he would be the furthest away from it.

Anas (*raḍiy-Allāh 'anhu*) remarked: "I served him for ten years and he never once rebuked me in the least; nor did he say about anything I had done: 'Why did you do it?' or anything I had not done: 'Why did you not to it?'"

His description (*ṣifah*) in the Torah is: "Muḥammad, the Messenger of Allāh and My Chosen Slave. He is neither harsh (*faẓẓ*) nor severe (*ghalīẓ*). He (ﷺ) does not shout in the market places, nor repay evil with evil, but instead he pardons and forgives."

His characteristic was that he (ﷺ)would be the first to greet those whom he met. If a person wanted to leave his gathering for a need, he would wait until that person left and he would not go before him.

If someone held his hand, he would not pull it back until the person who had held him released his hand.

He (ﷺ) would sit in an assembly wherever it was convenient, and he would mingle among his Companions as one of them, so much so that when a stranger came he would not be able to distinguish him from other, except after inquiring as to who he was. He (ﷺ) would take to long periods of silence; but when he did speak he did so slowly and clearly, repeating himself so that he would be clearly understood. He (ﷺ) used to pardon, even when he was in a position to punish, and he would not confront anyone with what they did not like.

He (ﷺ) was the most truthful of people; one who most fulfilled his commitments; the easiest going of people; the most pleasant; and the most generous of them in companionship. Whoever gazed upon him unexpectedly, would be awe-stricken by him; whoever associated with him and came to know him, loved him. His (ﷺ) Companions, whenever they spoke about worldly affairs, he would join in with them; and when, in recollecting their pre-Islāmic days, they would laugh, he would simply smile.

He (ﷺ) was the bravest of men; one Companion recalled: 'When the fighting became intense, we would seek shelter behind Allāh's Messenger (ﷺ).'

He (ﷺ) was not very tall or short, but he was of average height.

He (ﷺ) was complexion was ruddy and he was not dark skinned.

His (ﷺ) hair was even and well-combed. It was not long and curvy. His hair used to reach his lobes.

He (ﷺ) had a large forehead, concave eyebrows, dark-eyed, he had long eye lashes, and he had a high-tipped nose with thin nostrils. His cheeks were not bulky and he had a thick beard. He (ﷺ) had a high neck which gleamed like silver. He (ﷺ) was broad-shouldered, and his chest and stomach were in the same line (i.e., his stomach never protruded out of profile). He (ﷺ) had a broad chest and shoulders. His palm was softer than silk.

May Allāh's salutations and blessings be upon him.

Section Two:
A Summary Account of His (ﷺ) Miracles

Indeed a person who heard the condition of the Prophet (ﷺ) and heard his reports which contain his manners, actions, etiquettes, excellent administration of the interests of the people, his detailed explanation of the Sharīʿah which the intellectuals and eloquent people are incapable of; will have no doubt that these things were not acquired by stratagems, and it cannot be imagined that these things came from anywhere except from Allāh's help and power, and that cannot occur to a pretender or a liar. Rather his characteristics and condition are absolute testimonies of his truthfulness.

One of his (ﷺ) major miracles (*muʿjizat*) and clearest signs is the noble Qur'an, a creation impossible replicate. Every Prophet's miracle ended with his departure from the world, but the Qur'ān is an eternal miracle.

His (ﷺ) miracles included splitting the moon, the flowing of water from his fingers, his feeding of a large group of people from seemingly small amount of food, his throwing of a few pebbles which went into the eyes of many people, and the crying of the date-palm which cried for him like a pregnant camel that is about to give birth, and his information about future events and their occurrence as he had predicted. He (ﷺ) put back the eye of Qatādah (*raḍiy Allāh 'anhu*) which had come out of its socket with his own hands, and it became his best eye. He (ﷺ) also spat in the eyes of 'Alī (*raḍiy Allāh 'anhu*) when he had eye sore and he was immediately healed.

The Prophet (ﷺ) had other miracles which are well known and cannot be hidden. I ask Allāh to grant us the ability to follow his manners and characteristics. Indeed Allāh is Generous and He answers prayers, and all praise is due to Allāh.

www.ingramcontent.com/pod-product-compliance
Lightning Source LLC
Chambersburg PA
CBHW071849070526
44583CB00016B/1607
* 9 7 8 1 6 4 3 5 4 4 7 3 1 *